GARDNER

VOL. III
ATHLETES AND AUTHORS

COREY GARDNER

GARDNER

GARDNER is the name on my grandfather's tombstone and as I stood there, I said to myself, "That name stands for something." A man's surname is his Y – chromosome. It is passed from father to son, from generation to generation. A man's surname is his mark, his reputation, and his legacy. It is a man's duty to protect the honor of the family name.

It came from your father,
It was all he had to give,
So it's yours to use and cherish
As long as you may live.
If you lose the watch he gave you,
It can always be replaced,
But a black mark on your name, son,
Can never be erased.
It was clean the day you took it
And a worthy name to bear.
When I got it from my father
There was no dishonor there.
So make sure you guard it wisely –
After all is said and done,
You'll be glad the name is spotless
When you give it to your son.

- Anonymous

GARDNER

Vol. III: Athletes and Authors

COREY GARDNER

ISBN: 978 – 1 – 7339298 – 3 – 7

Contact information:
GARDNERCA89@aol.com
GARDNERsurname@aol.com
GARDNERbook@gmail.com

Corey Gardner

ACKNOWLEDGEMENTS

Larry Gardner and Jenny Gardner, my parents, for always being there.

Leroy Gardner, a distant cousin, author of _GARDNER/BALLARD and ALLIED FAMILIES_, for being a great genealogist who has passed on the torch of becoming the Gardner family historian.

Brady Cloud, U. S. Marine and U. S. Army soldier, for being a great friend and mentor, along with being a sparring partner in boxing.

Tony Gardner, the "KO King", the NABF Jr. Middleweight Champion, for being part of this book.

John L. Gardner, the Heavyweight Champion of Great Britain, the Commonwealth, and Europe, for being part of this book.

Tyrone Gardiner, the Lightweight Champion of Canada, for being part of this book.

GARDNER
Vol. I: Commandos and War Heroes
Corey Gardner

GARDNER Vol. I: Commandos and War Heroes contains over 40 biographies on warriors, mercenaries, knights, commandos, and war heroes surnamed Gardner. They range from Confederate generals to fighter pilots to Navy SEALs, ranging from war heroes of the American Revolution to the Civil War to both of the World Wars, Vietnam, Iraq, and Afghanistan all with the last name Gardner. It lists all the brave men who died in Vietnam and Iraq, biographies on the bravest men who served their country on battlefields all over the world with the proud family surname Gardner.

GARDNER
Vol. I: Commandos and War Heroes
Chapter I: Warriors, Mercenaries, and Knights
Gardner
Sir Osborn Gardner, Knight of Jerusalem
Sir Wyllyam Gardner, the Assassin of King Richard III
Sir Christopher Gardner, Knight of the Holy Sepulchre
Lion Gardner, America's First Hero
Col. Jas. Gardner, the Christian Hero
Admiral Alan Gardner, the 1st Baron Gardner
Col. William Linneaus Gardner, the Cavalry Officer
Col. Alexander Gardner, the Mercenary

Chapter II: Commandos and War Heroes
Col. Thomas Gardner, the Revolutionary War Hero
Carswell Gardner, the Bodyguard of the Washington Family
Capt. Thomas Gardner, the Privateer
Gen. Sir Robert Gardner, the British Artillery Officer
Sgt. Maj. William Gardner, the Scottish Warrior
Colour Sgt. George Gardner, the Irish Warrior
Col. Charles Gardner, the Hero of the War of 1812
Maj. Gen. Franklin Gardner, the Confederate General
Brig. Gen. William Montgomery Gardner, the Southern Gentleman
Lt. Col. Robert D. Gardner, the Confederate Officer
Sgt. Tom Gardner, the Confederate Cavalryman
Pvt. Billy Gardner, the Rebel Sharpshooter
Brig. Gen. John Lane Gardner, the Union Officer
Maj. Asa Gardner, the Yankee Officer
Capt. Joseph Gardner, the Freedom Fighter
Sgt. Barnard Gardner, the Yankee Sniper
Pvt. Peter Gardner, the Yankee Soldier
Commander Frank Gardner, the Sailor
Capt. Cecil Gardner, the Fighter Pilot
Capt. George Gardner, the Flying Ace
Capt. Percy Gardner, the Canadian Warrior

2nd Lt. Cyril Gardner, the World War I Hero
1st Sgt. John H. Gardner, the American Warrior
Col. Larry Gardner, the Aviator
Maj. Madison D. Gardner, U. S. Army Soldier
Capt. Phillip Gardner, the Victoria Cross Recipient
Capt. William A. Gardner, the American Ace
1st Sgt. Garviss Lee Gardner, U. S. Army Sniper
Sgt. Frank Gardner, U. S. Marine
Cpl. Cliff Gardner, the World War II Hero
Alvy Gardner, the UDT Operator
Lt. Russ Gardner, the Canadian Officer
Meredith Knox Gardner, the Cold War Hero
Capt. Alan Gardner, the Green Beret
Capt. Gregory Gardner, U. S. Army Ranger
1st Lt. Jim Gardner, U. S. Army Ranger
Lt. Bill Gardner, U. S. Navy SEAL
Master Chief Bud Gardner, U. S. Navy SEAL
Master Chief Jason Gardner, U. S. Navy SEAL
Vietnam War Heroes, 9/11 Heroes, Iraq War Heroes, and Medal of Honor Recipients

GARDNER
Vol. II: Cowboys and Gunslingers
Corey Gardner

GARDNER Vol. II: Cowboys and Gunslingers contains over 30 biographies on cowboys, gunslingers, outlaws, and lawmen surnamed Gardner. The volume has bad men and good men, who lived on the outside of the law and the men who enforced the law, including a list of fallen heroes who died in the line of duty to serve and protect. They range from mountain men of the Rockies to Indian fighters on the frontier to deadly gunfighters surnamed Gardner.

GARDNER
Vol. II: Cowboys and Gunslingers
Chapter III: Cowboys and Indian Fighters

Johnson Gardner, the Mountain Man
Big Phil Gardner, the Desperado
Thomas Gardner, the Arizona Pioneer
Alfred Gardner, the Texas Ranger
Arizona Bill Gardner, the Army Scout
Col. John H. Gardner, the Cavalryman
Dan Gardner, the Texas Cattleman
John Gardner, the American Cowboy
Joe Gardner, the World Roping Champion
George Gardner, the Wild West Performer
Clem Gardner, the Rodeo Star

Chapter IV: Gunslingers

Lewis Gardner, the Gunfighter
Pliny Gardner, the Pistoleer
Lige Gardner, the Texas Pistolero
Tom Gardner, the Fastest Gun Alive
Charles Gardner, the Colorado Kid
Jeremiah Gardner, the Plainsman
Maynard Gardner, the Mississippi Gunslinger
Buck Gardner, the Texas Bad Man
Roll Gardner, the Rifleman
Matt Gardner, the Shootist
The Gardner Gang
Gunslingin' Gardners

Chapter V: Outlaws

Roy Gardner, the Outlaw
Johnny Gardner, the Gangster
Peck Gardner, the Mob Boss of East Chicago
Bud Gardner, the Mobster
Roger Gardner, the Most Wanted Fugitive
Ronnie Lee Gardner, the Convicted Killer
Death Row Inmates

Chapter VI: Lawmen

GARDNER
Vol. III: Athletes and Authors
Corey Gardner

GARDNER Vol. III: Athletes and Authors contains over 20 biographies on prize – fighters, athletes, politicians, authors, and entertainers surnamed Gardner. They range from a British boxing champion to an American wrestling champion to a Hollywood actress to a spy novelist. The volume has all of those who stepped into the spotlight onto a stage or in a ring surnamed Gardner.

Chapter VII: Prize – Fighters

"**Boxing is a manly sport. Every boy should have to take part in it to some extent. It knocks the bully out of him and makes him respect the other fellow.**" – Jack Gardner

AWFUL GARDNER

Awful Gardner, the Prize – Fighter, was one of the most feared and famous men in America. He was the Mike Tyson of the 19th Century, even once biting a man's ear off in a fight. Gardner was a famous fighter and notorious gangster on the streets of New York City, earning even more notoriety when he became one of America's first celebrities to convert to Christianity.

"If there was anyone worse than he was I never heard of him or read of him." – Broadbrim's New York Letter, *Wanganui Chronicle*

"The great religious revivals of 1858, were marked by the conversion of a prize – fighter whose name was known among sporting men, from one end of the country to the other. This was Orville Gardner, whose fistic prowess had been the means of having his first name changed in common speech among his associates from Orville, to 'Awful'."

"Awful" Gardner was the **"celebrated prize – fighter of Newark City"** and was undefeated at one time.

Gardner was described as being over six feet tall and powerfully – built, even in advanced years, according to a newspaper reporter. **"He was a broad shouldered, burly individual, with a tremendous neck, and an arm as thick as a moderate sized man's leg. His career had been notorious and infamous in the extreme, he having been one of the roughs employed by politicians, and engaged in rows and fights without number, figuring several times in the prize – ring, and once having bitten off a man's nose!"**

Hezekiah Orville Gardner was born in 1825 in New York. The Gardner family removed in 1836 to Newark, New Jersey and his father was Hezekiah Gardner, a dairy man from Newburgh, New York. The elder Gardner fathered ten children:

John C. Gardner, a shoemaker who later fought in the Civil War.
Orville "Awful" Gardner, a notorious prizefighter, gambler, and ruffian.
"Horrible" Howell E. Gardner, a notorious prizefighter and evangelist preacher.
Margaret Gardner, wife of Joseph H. Miller, a printer and newspaper editor.
Elijah Francisco Gardner, a journeyman who later fought in the Civil War.
Ellen Gardner, twin sister of Elijah.
Frederick Bigler Gardner, a silverplater.
Deselding "Seldon" Gardner, a policeman.
Mary E. Gardner, twin sister of Deselding.
Freeborn G. Gardner, a silverplater and later stove paper store clerk.

According to his own story, Gardner killed a man named Jim Morris with a body slam in a street fight. He fled to New York City where he began his career as an emigrant runner, he married Amelia Doty on May 9th, 1844, and they had two children. Gardner was a member of the Bowery Boys, an infamous street gang, running errands and roughing up immigrants.

Orville "Awful" Gardner defeated Allen McFee, the Scottish heavyweight champion, after 33 rounds in 1847 in a prize – fight. It is said he was undefeated for a long time until he was supposedly defeated in a prize – fight with "Yankee" Sullivan and earned his nickname. Gardner claimed his only loss was in 1853 after 17 rounds to Bill Hastings, alias "Dublin Tricks" and it was during the early 1850s that he was involved in several barroom brawls.

On February 21st, 1851, *The Sun* (Baltimore, Maryland) reported:
"Man shot by Awful Gardner will probably not recover. He is lodged in prison to await trial result."

On May 4th, 1852, the front page of *The New York Times* reported:

A fight took place on Sunday night at the oyster saloon of Van Name & Bush near the Museum on Broadway. "Awful" Gardner beat some of the party severely and made his exit. Four men were arrested by police.

Aside from being a ruffian, Gardner was a distinguished boxing trainer. He trained such American heavyweight champions as Tom Hyer, John Morrissey, and Joe Coburn. It was noted that Gardner held Yankee Sullivan's arms back and allowed John Morrissey to win the Heavyweight Championship of America.

On October 14th, 1853, Orville "Awful" Gardner was arrested for assaulting another prize – fighter named William Hastings, alias "Dublin Tricks". According to newspapers, Gardner knocked Hastings down after an argument, and bit his ear off. Afterwards, he was arrested while stepping aboard a Philadelphia train.

On October 17th, 1853, *The New York Times* reported:

THE PRIZE – FIGHTERS
ARREST OF "AWFUL GARDNER"
More Battles in this City and Staten Island

On Friday, October 14th, 1853, Orville "Awful" Gardner struck William Hastings, alias "Dublin Tricks", knocking him down and biting his left ear, biting a large piece off, as well as trying to gouge his right eye out. Gardner fled to New Jersey, but was arrested by police as he was boarding the Philadelphia train, being charged with assault and battery.

Fun and Fancy in Old New York: Reminiscences of a Man about Town by Tom Piction and William L. Slout reads:

"Among those enthusiasts of native origin carried away by a desire to flourish in the roped arena came Orville, or Awful Gardner, a young man who had already signalized himself in different street brawls, principally brought about in consequence of his business, that of an emigrant runner, bringing him in contact with a troublesome and quarrelsome class of the community. Awful made his first appearance in a ring in a contest with McTee, the Scottish Champion, whom he defeated in a sharp rattling mill. During this Gardner met with an irreparable injury in the loss of the fore joint of a finger, broken in the delivery of a knock down blow.

Notwithstanding this misfortune, Gardner afterwards met William Hastings, surnamed "Dublin Tricks", when, after a couple of rounds, his mutilated hand became useless. Defeated by Hastings, Gardner withdrew from the ring and resumed his usual occupation. His pugilistic tendencies soon got him into difficulties and, convicted of an assault, he was sent to the penitentiary, whence all the importunities of his friends were unable to obtain his release, so strong was the prejudice of the authorities against him."

However, in 1854, the turning point in his life was when his son, Orville Gardner, age 6, died after drowning.

The Dangerous Classes of New York by Charles Loring Brace reads:

"The point through which his brutalized nature had been touched, had been evidently his affection for an only child – a little boy. He described to me once, in very simple, touching language, his affection and love for this child; how he dressed him in the best, and did all he could for him, but always keeping him away from all knowledge of his own dissipation. One day he was off on some devilish errand among the immigrants on Staten Island, when he saw a boat approaching quickly with one of his "pals". The man rowed up near him, and stopped and looked at him "very queer," and didn't say anything.

"What the devil are you looking at me in that way for?" said Gardner. "Your boy is drowned!" replied the other.

"Gardner says he fell back in the boat, as if you'd hit him right straight from the shoulder behind the ear, and did not know anything for a long time. When he recovered, he kept himself drunk for three weeks, and smashed a number of policemen, and was "put up," just so as to forget the bright little fellow who had been the pride of his heart."

On October 3rd, 1855, *The New York Times* reported:

AWFUL GARDNER SENTENCED FOR SIX MONTHS

Hezekiah Orville "Awful" Gardner was indicted for assault on John Henry of Utica. According to witnesses, Gardner attempted to persuade Henry to go to a house kept by a Mr. Chamberlain. After Mr. Henry refused, Gardner knocked him down, breaking his jaw – bone with his fist.

Gardner was arrested and sentenced to six months in the penitentiary.

He attended the funeral of his friend, the notorious William Poole, also known as "Bill the Butcher", who had been fatally shot in 1855 in a theatre. The film titled, "Gangs of New York" portrays actor Daniel Day – Lewis as gangster "Bill the Butcher". After the death of his son, it seems Gardner caused as much trouble as before, but he would soon see the light.

According to a newspaper, "Awful" Gardner was a contender for the Heavyweight Championship of America in 1856 against Dominick Bradley. The odds were in favor of Gardner. It is unknown whether or not he ever won or competed for a championship title, but it is likely, due to the fact that he had a celebrated career as a prize – fighter.

It was during the religious revivals of 1858, that he converted to Christianity. Accounts vary, but the main story is that Gardner was standing outside of a saloon and looking up at the sky, he said to himself, "I wonder where my little boy is tonight?" Then the thought came to him, "Wherever he is, you will never see him again unless you change your life."

"A noted pugilist, a profligate man whose name was familiar to the city in the annals of violence and wrong," Gardner was on bail pending a charge of assault and battery in Hoboken when he was converted.

The Testimony of Orville "Awful" Gardner:
"I felt it my duty to tell you what God has done for me. I hope you will hear all I have to say. There are many here who have known me for ten years – have known me when I was fearfully wicked. Now I am on the Lord's side. I want it thoroughly understood that now I am on the Lord's side.

I was on a visit to my brother in the country, about twenty eight miles away, at a town called Portchester. When I went there I had as much idea of getting religion as many of you have now –that is none at all. But I hope when you get home you cannot rest nor sleep till you get religion. I went to church in that town for accommodation, that's all, to the folks. The Savior was there. The Lord's Spirit was powerfully displayed, and went from heart to heart all through the church. It worked upon me three

or four nights. The pastor of the church came to me and asked me if I would not like to get religion and serve God. I answered, 'No I didn't care about it just then,' and told him a lie, for I did. I felt as though I wanted religion.

I got dreadfully uneasy, and made up my mind I had better leave that part of the country; it was getting too warm for me. I told my brother I was going to New York in the morning. He said, 'Wait another day,' and I made up my mind I would stay and attend another night. [He attended meetings at the church on Friday and Saturday, but felt no relief.]

I got up and threw my sins down by the altar. I tried as hard as a man ever did, and I got no religion.

Sunday night I attended with a like result. That night I could not sleep, my sins looked so bad; they came up on every hand and looked at me; all the sins of my life crowded upon me, many I should never have thought of, had not the devil brought them before me. I could not sleep; I wiggled and waggled around the bed all night; the Lord was striving with me.

Monday morning I got up and prayed; I did the best I could; I asked the Lord to take away the weight that bore me down so. There was a friend came to me that day and said he was going over to White Plains, and I could go with him. Knowing I would be in good company, I concluded to go, thinking he might do me some good. There was little said on the way, but he told me to keep looking for the Savior; that I was trying to get religion and let everybody know it; the Lord was willing to bless me at any time or anywhere.

I was riding along, singing a hymn, and in an instant I felt as though I was blessed. I am sure I gave up my soul and body. The first thing I knew, God spoke peace to my soul. It came like a shot – it came like lightning, when I was not anticipating it, and the first thing I said, "Glory! God blessed me."

My friend said he knew it; he felt the shock too. We rode against a stone fence two or three times, and came near tumbling to the ground. The change was surprising; the trees looked as if they had been blessed; everything appeared to have been blessed, even the horse and wagon. I felt strong. I could almost fly. Glory to God, this religion is good! The Lord has blessed me ever since. My faith in him grows stronger every day. I would face all the people that God ever put on the earth, and tell them all I am bound for heaven. My heart says, see the scorner: I say, I will go pray for him. Everything is pleasing. I love those I used to hate.

Now, that shows pretty good for religion – don't it, brothers? [Yes, yes.] Men that I used to seek to injure I love now; I pray for them. I don't hate a soul that God ever put breath in...I would not swap this religion for all New York City. I would rather have religion and live on bread and water till God calls me. I have tasted the world's pleasures, but religion is the only thing that will make a man happy here, and the only thing that will make him happy hereafter. There are a great many here that know me,

and it is, no doubt, a mystery to them that God should accept such a creature.

Now is the time to step to the altar. Don't say to God, let me accomplish this or that, and then I will seek you. When you receive the religion of Jesus Christ you are the richest person on the earth. Come at once. Clear the way, here! Seats all around; allow yourselves to be led to Christ."

As he was touched by the Spirit of God, he began to pray and gave up drinking. He began the "Coffee and Reading Room", also known as "The Drunkards' Club" in the worst district of the city, the Fourth Ward. Orville Gardner was the leader of one of the first AA meetings.

It was during a powerful sermon in the 1860s at the Sing Sing Prison that he helped convert young Irish convict Jerry McAuley, who later created his own mission for troubled youths.

The notorious ruffian, bare – knuckle fighter, gambler, and rough, Orville "Awful" Gardner, was a mighty preacher of Christianity. It was in 1879 that a newspaper reporter interviewed Gardner. The 54 – year old man told his life story.

On Thursday, November 22nd, 1877, the front page of the *Wilkes – Barre Leader* (Wilkes – Barre, Pennsylvania) Volume II, Issue 19, headlined:

Awful Gardner's Story. How a rumseller and Prize Fighter Became a Christian and Temperance Orator

"A report was published yesterday that Orville Gardner, once a prize fighter, but for nearly twenty years a zealous Christian and temperance orator, was about to open a saloon in Newark, that he might, by rumselling, gain in his old age, enfeebled by disease and forsaken by his friends, that livelihood which he was no longer able to get consistently with his principles. A world reporter visited the old man in his humble home on Saturday to learn if the report was true.

Gardner is a very powerfully built man, over six feet tall, and fifty – four years old, but erect and vigorous looking. The appearance was, however, deceptive, for a stroke of paralysis eight years ago robbed him of the strength of his manhood, and he has been until lately a cripple from its effects."

"My father was born in Newburg," he said, "and after living in Newark he went back there and died. My mother was acquainted in Newburg and came here with her family to live. There were not many of us, only fifteen brothers and sisters."

"Well, as we boys grew up we got to going out and working for ourselves. I was a pretty lively boy, and I used to be on the street a good deal. I used to swell round on Broad street and Market street, and I thought I was a man when I was about seventeen years old. One night Jim Dennison came to me – he was one of the captains of the place, captain of a sort of military organization – and said, "You are a good deal too smart. If I catch you putting on airs around the corner of Market and Broad streets, I'll give you a licking." I said, "Very well, do it if you can and I won't say anything about it."

"You see he was a man and I was only a boy, and I had never done any fighting to amount to anything. Id' been round fighting boys a good deal and I'd whipped a school master once, but no real fighting."

"Well, one word led to another and we fought it out then and there, and I whaled him – gave him a good whaling."

About three months after this I was in a little sort of a gin – shop and domino shop and card – shop on Market street and Jim Morris came in. He was a cousin of Jim Dennison and a sporting man, about twenty – six years old.

He said to me, "You are getting too smart, going round whipping everybody. You'd better look out, or I'll give you the damndest licking you ever had."

I said, "You are a man and I am a boy. Go and talk to a man."

Well, he kept on talking and I was pretty saucy, so one word led to another and at last he kicked me.

I didn't allow anybody, man or boy, to kick me then, and I told him so, and I said: "If you come up stairs we will settle it now."

So we went up stairs and had a fight. We fought for a considerable time, and finally the crowd came in and told us to go outside and finish the fight.

We fought clear across the street and over on the other sidewalk, and I threw him down again.

I could throw any of 'em in those days when I caught him 'cross the butt as I did him, and the last time he fell on his back on the curbstone and hurt himself.

We went home, and they talked of arresting me, so I kept out of the way. Then they began to say he might die, and I started to run away. I got as far as the depot, when they arrested me and took me before 'Squire Andrews – Nune Andrews, we called him – I don't know what his name was – and they talked of sending me to State prison.

Well, poor Jim Morris did die from the effects of the injury he had received in the fight, and it would have gone hard with me but a number of prominent citizens came forward – men who stood high in the community, and Jim Dennison was among 'em, too – and said I wasn't to blame.

They said that Morris had picked the fight with me and I wasn't to blame, so I got off. Nune Andrews said to me: "You miserable young blackguard, you ought to be locked up anyway. Newark is no place for you." I said, "If you will let me go I will leave Newark', and he let me go on that condition.

"Then I went to New York and first went into the rum business. Then I got into emigrant running, for I was a great fighter and there was a good deal of fighting in that business. We would have lively fights, and sometimes the captains of the ships would call up the sailors to stop the fighting.

Well, I got into fighting pretty extensively. I went up the Troy and got a hold of John Morrissey and brought him out. I trained him for his fight with Yankee Sullivan and was his second. And I brought out Tom Hyer and trained him. He was the best man with his fists that ever fought on this continent.

I was mixed up in all the fights in those days, and at election times Bill Poole, and John Morrissey and 'Awful' Gardner and such men had it all their own way.

We would make bargains – "You do this for me, and I'll do that for you' – and we'd have anybody elected that we wanted.

'Then I was in the ring twice. I don't count fights that would be made up in private for a few baskets of wine or for a barrel of whiskey or something like that, but real public fights for money.

The first fight was with Allen McFee, a Scotchman, and the second was with Dublin Tricks – Bill Hastings, his real name was.

That was the only fight I ever lost, and I think I might have won that one if it hadn't been for my backers. They kept me back in the fighting till they should have their outside bets all made. I wasn't to fight till I should see a man in the opposite corner wave a red handkerchief.

So I never struck a blow the first part of the fight, and at length be struck a terrible blow that I warded off with my left arm. The force was so great, though, that when I threw my arm up I threw it clear out of joint. After that I went on for three rounds with my left arm hanging useless at my side.

I couldn't use it, of course, and I couldn't do anything but strike out with my right arm and use my head for a guard as well as I could.

I think I might have whipped my man even that way, for I got in one body – blow that almost knocked him out of time; but after three rounds my backers – those that had their money in the stakes – jumped into the ring and stopped the fight.

CONVERSION

"Then I was taken sick and went on to Morristown, and was under the doctor's care for eight months. I had a large tumor under my skull right on the brain, and it has affected my mind. The doctor said it was as large as a hen's egg. I suppose it came from some of the bruises on my head that I had got in fighting."

"I have been a special policeman here in Newark for a number of years, and I have made more important arrests than any other man on the force. They used to pay me for my arrests, so much for each one."

"I have had a good many offers to go into the rum business as barkeeper. A good many people would be glad to have Orville Gardner in their places, for it would draw customers."

It seems "Awful" Gardner was a "special policeman" in Newark, New Jersey, collecting rewards as a bounty hunter.

On Saturday, June 30th, 1877, *The Pioche Weekly Record* (Pioche, Nevada) recorded his brother Rev. Howell Gardner making a statement of his brother Orville Gardner sounding more like a Western gunfighter than a New York City prizefighter.

Howell Gardner recalled a story of Orville Gardner killing a Long Island hotel keeper who pointed a gun at him after an argument. Newspapers insisted that the Gardners killed a dozen people on Long Island. And finally, the reverend stated that his brother, "Awful" Gardner knocked out a man named O' Brien, breaking his jaw and killing him. His friends, being longshoremen, found Orville Gardner staying at the American House in Williamsburg where they tried to kill him. However, Gardner drew his revolver and shot three of them.

He later retired to a quiet place in New Jersey due to his health, but he was back to his old ways. Afterwards, he was kicked out of a home. Then, his wife, Amelia died in 1890 at the Old Women's Home in Metuchen, New Jersey.

On March 20th, 1889, *The New York Times* reported:

ORVILLE GARDNER INSANE.

On March 19th, 1889, in New Brunswick, New Jersey, Orville Gardner was sent to the State insane asylum at 62 years old. According to the news article, Gardner was about 60 years old in 1887 and encountered a party of young men on the street. Gardner whipped all five of them and put the others to flight within five minutes.

Broadbrim's New York letter in 1890 featured an Australian newspaper, *Wanganui Chronicle* reported:

"Fifty years ago there was bruiser in New York whose very name was a terror among fighting men – he was known as Awful Gardner. His name was Orville. In those days that name meant something; for every engine – house was a school for knocking out, and the prize ring was the high road to preferment. John Morrissey reached Congress, and John Heenan could have died rich. Yankee Sullivan stood about as high as the Mayor, while Bill Harrington, Abe Vanderzee, Tom Hyer and Dutch Charley were regarded by most of our youthful citizens as indefinitely better men than the Judges of the Supreme Court. It was in this desperate crowd that Awful Gardner earned his name, and held it against all comers for years. If there was anyone worse than he was I never heard of him or read of him."

It is unknown what happened to the feared prizefighter turned mighty preacher, but it is said that he died from an illness in 1899 in New Jersey.

References:
The New York Times
The Sun
The Dangerous Classes of New York by Charles Loring Brace
Every where..., Volumes 17-18 edited by Will Carleton
Fun and Fancy in Old New York: Reminiscences of a Man about Town by Tom Piction and William L. Slout

OSCAR GARDNER

Oscar Gardner, the "Omaha Kid", was the Featherweight Champion of America. He was one of the greatest featherweights of his era. Gardner fought for the Featherweight Championship of the World four times during his career.

"I haven't time to train. I am so busy fighting that I get on and off trains and just have time to get into the ring. If I didn't drink beer or ale or do something to sustain me, I wouldn't be able to whip anybody in the country. My wind has no time to go bad. It is a sort of continuous performance with me. One fight makes me fit and ready for the next one. I have a system of my own." – Oscar Gardner

He only stood 5' 3 ½ and weighed anywhere from 115 to 125 pounds, but he was no joke. Gardner once killed a man in the ring; he was tough, confident, and game. "The Omaha Kid" had a good chin, fast hands and feet, ring savvy, and knockout power, especially against his fellow featherweights; his only weakness were his brittle hands, which he broke seven times during his career, causing him to lose matches he might have won.

Oscar Desire Gardner was born on May 19th, 1872, a native of Minneapolis, Minnesota. He began working at a mattress plant and began training as a pugilist at Professor Downer's Gymnasium. Gardner later moved to Sioux City, Iowa, with friends looking for adventure and began working at another mattress factory and he would often box with his fellow co – workers.

During an interview, he stated:
"It's funny the way I started fighting," said Oscar Gardner recently.

"I was born in Minneapolis, May 19, 1872, and when 14 years old had a job in a mattress factory in Omaha, Neb. During the noon hour we used to slip on the boxing gloves for a few rounds.

Among the fellows with whom I used to box was Jack Davis, who had earned a name for himself as a pugilist. One day after I had given him a stiff argument, he asked me why I didn't adopt prize fighting as a profession.

I thought he was 'kidding' me, but he told me he was in earnest. He mentioned a young fellow by the name of John Cordon, from Nebraska City, who was looking for a match.

In a jest I asked how much the loser would get and Davis replied $35. That amount of money looked big to me and I jumped at it.

I trained hard, and to the surprise of everybody, including myself, defeated Cordon in seven rounds. I was then 15."

Gardner made his debut as a professional fighter in 1887 in Omaha, Nebraska, defeating John Cordon by 7 – Round KO, although some reports state the fight was in August of 1891, and that his first fight was a 5 – Round KO victory over Alfred Hamilton in Sioux City, Iowa.

On August 11th, 1892, Gardner defeated Jim Porter, 2 – 3, by 22 – Round KO for the Featherweight Championship of the Northwest in Minneapolis, Minnesota.

"How did I come by the name of "Omaha Kid"? Well you see it was this way:

When I went to Omaha, my mother remained in Minneapolis. I didn't want her to know I was fighting and when I returned to the Mill City in 1891, I was offered a match with Jimmy Porter before a Minneapolis boxing club.

I told the club management not to mention my real name, but to use any other name seen fit, and so they dubbed me, "The Omaha Kid," which name has stuck with me ever since."

On September 1st, 1892, Gardner knocked out two men in one night. He defeated Scotty Gordon by 9 – Round TKO and Harley Davis by 4 – Round TKO, both of which were in Omaha, Nebraska. "The Omaha Kid" was 6 – 0 (6 KO's) and went the distance for the first time, winning an 8 – Round Decision over Eddie Schulenberg in St. Paul, Minnesota.

On May 8th, 1893, Gardner defeated contender Solly Smith, 13 – 0 (11 KO's) by 6 – Round Decision.

On June 10th, 1893, Gardner defeated Solly Smith, 13 – 1 (11 KO's), in a rematch and knocked out Smith in 6 rounds, leaving no doubt he was a contender.

He boxed around Omaha for a couple of years, then in St. Paul where he fought Solly Smith who was reputed to be the lightweight champion.

Gardner stated:
"He agreed to stop me inside of six rounds, but the conclusion of the bout found me waiting for more. I outpointed Smith, and it was then my fortune in the ring was made, for I was the receiver of challenges from all sides."

On July 31st, 1893, Oscar Gardner, 12 – 0 – 1 (10 KO's), fought Tommy Dixon, 8 – 0 – 1 (6 KO's), for the Featherweight Championship of the Northwest. He lost by 13 – Round KO in St. Paul, Minnesota. It was his first loss.

He later gained more experience after fighting a grueling 41 – Round Draw against Johnny Van Heest, 40 – 3 – 6, along with several KO victories.

Gardner defeated Eddie Thompson by 1 – Round KO and put Jimmy Evans away in 3 rounds.

On May 26th, 1895, "The Omaha Kid" fought Tommy Dixon, 10 – 0 – 3, in a rematch for the Featherweight Championship of America, held outside a cornfield in Kansas City, Kansas. Dixon was knocked through the ropes in the second round. Gardner was down in the 14th, 28th, 34th, 35th, and 36th rounds, his seconds throwing in the sponge, losing by 36 – Round TKO.

Then on March 13th, 1897, Gardner lost to Solly Smith, 21 – 5, by 20 – Round Decision.

On April 10th, 1897, "The Omaha Kid" defeated veteran and contender, "Torpedo" Billy Murphy, 84 – 31, by 20 – Round Decision in New York, New York.

On September 15th, 1897, Oscar Gardner, 34 – 4, defeated the undefeated Tommy Dixon, 17 – 0, by 20 – Round Decision at the National Athletic Club in Rochester, New York in their third fight.

"The Omaha Kid" knocked out the likes of Johnny Van Heest in 11 rounds and Luke Stevens in 6 rounds, along with fighting a 20 – Round Draw with Patsy Haley.

On April 7th, 1898, Oscar Gardner defeated George Stout by 12 – Round KO at Wirthwein's Hall in Cincinnati, Ohio. It was in the 12th round, Gardner landed a straight right that landed flush on the chin of Stout, knocking him out cold. Reports state it sounded **"like the crack of a pistol shot"** when his head hit the ground, dying from his injuries due to a blood clot at the base of the brain.

On Saturday, April 9th, 1898, *Omaha World Herald* reported:
Omaha Kid Kills. Oscar Gardner and Seconds Held for Murder

On December 8th, 1898, *The Reading Eagle* reported: **"Oscar Gardner was today acquitted at Columbus on the charge of prize fighting. An attempt was made to indict Gardner for manslaughter, but unsuccessfully."**

"The Omaha Kid" had a winning streak of 20 straight wins, 16 by knockout, with a handful of draws in between.

On June 30th, 1898, Gardner defeated Jack McClelland, 16 – 0, by 10 – Round KO, handing him his first loss.

On October 28th, 1898, Gardner defeated former World Bantamweight Champion Sammy Kelly, 16 – 3, by 14 – Round KO for the Featherweight Championship of America in New York City.

As the number one contender, he earned his title shot.

On November 29th, 1898, at age 26, Oscar Gardner fought African – American World Featherweight Champion, George Dixon, 47 – 5 – 25, at Lenox Athletic Club in New York City, New York, for the Featherweight Championship of the World.

He lost by 25 – Round Decision, the crowd booing and hissing the decision, and it was the consensus among writers that Gardner had won without question.

Dixon's manager ran the Lenox Athletic Club and it was he who hand – picked the referee that night. After the fight, Dixon was recorded as having walked into Oscar's dressing room and said, "Oscar, I don't want you to think that I had anything to do with that decision tonight. I have the winner's end of the purse, and if you want any part of it, it is yours for the asking."

On February 14th, 1899, *Evening Telegraph* reported:
"In disposition Gardner is quiet and unassuming. He likes to fight and believes that square tactics pay. He is not a stickler for conditions governing his contests, but says he can box "any old way."

Gardner knocked out the likes of Dave Sullivan and Solly Smith, having earned himself another title shot.

On February 8th, 1899, *The New York Times* reported:
"SOLLY" SMITH KNOCKED OUT.; Oscar Gardner, "the Omaha Kid," an Easy Victor in the Boxing Match at the Lenox Athletic Club."

On February 22nd, 1899, Oscar Gardner fought a 20 – Round Draw against Martin Flaherty, 21 – 7 – 16, at the Coliseum in Hartford, Connecticut. It was described as an excellent fight at 126 pounds. The fight was advertised as the Featherweight Championship of the World.

Gardner put together a string of victories, and again, he was in line for a title shot.

On March 9th, 1900, Oscar Gardner fought "Terrible" Terry McGovern, 42 – 2, for the World Featherweight Title at the Broadway Athletic Club in New York City.

Gardner floored McGovern in the first round, knocking him out with a counter hook. As he stood over him, McGovern grabbed his leg and refused to let go. Gardner tried to pull away and fell down, crying "Foul". The referee refused to disqualify the champion.

It was a highly controversial 16 second long count that was actually a first round knockout victory.

Sadly, the "Omaha Kid" lost by 3 – Round KO, an uncrowned champion.

Gardner put together another string of victories. He defeated Patsy Haley, 23 – 16, by 5 – Round KO in Shawnee, Ohio, and "The Omaha Kid" defeated Eddie Santry, 23 – 5, by 5 – Round KO in Louisville, Kentucky.

On June 1st, 1900, Oscar Gardner defeated Harry Forbes, 40 – 5, the future Bantamweight Champion of the World, by 1 – Round KO at the Star Theatre in Chicago, Illinois, perhaps his best victory.

On October 8th, 1900, he fought Tommy Dixon for a fourth time, losing by 14 – Round TKO due to the referee reportedly holding Oscar Gardner's arms behind his back, allowing Dixon to hit him.

He had a mixed career of losses and draws, but while on the decline of his career at only 29, he had his last title shot.

On April 30th, 1901, Oscar Gardner fought "Terrible" Terry McGovern, 51 – 2, for the World Featherweight Title at Mechanic's Pavilion in San Francisco, California, again knocking out McGovern who was again allowed to recover by the referee, "The Omaha Kid" losing by 4 – KO with a right hand, left hook.

Gardner stated:
"When I met Terry McGovern in Chicago, several years ago, I beat him fairly and squarely, but the house was betting against me, and the referee did not dare to give me the decision.

> In the fourth round of the contest I knocked McGovern stiff, and thinking the referee had him counted out, started for my corner. The "Brooklyn Terror," although he became very tame after I hit him, was carried to his chair and given plenty of time to recover from the effects of the blow.
>
> I was astonished when the referee called us from our corners and told us to continue the battle.
>
> In fact I was so enraged at the idea that I struck the referee and put him to the had.
>
> The rest of the story of the fight is easily told. McGovern managed to 'cop' me with an awful swing and I was turned from a winner into a loser."

After four more losses and a draw, he retired that same year. His record is listed as 87 – 18 – 32 (61 KO's), a total of 138 fights. Historians today record his number of fights as 86 – 21 – 34 (59 KO's).

Gardner and his managers reported his ring record was 472 wins, 42 losses, and 23 draws. He had a total of 537 fights. His obituary later stated he had 547 ring battles. *The Evening Telegraph* reported:

> "Gardner is the hero of 527 battles, of which twenty – three were draws and fifteen he lost.
>
> George Dixon, the ex – featherweight champion, is the only man who has fought more times than the Omaha boy.
>
> One of his most remarkable encounters was that with George Dixon, when the colored boy held the featherweight championship.
>
> Dixon was then reputed as invincible, but Gardner held him even for twenty – five rounds. The decision was given to Dixon.
>
> Gardner fought three championship battles in one month, an incident unsurpassed in ring annals. The men he met were George Dixon, Terry McGovern, featherweight, and Sammy Kelly, bantamweight, all of whom held world's titles when he faced them."

He worked as a security guard in Portland, Oregon, married, and fathered a son, later moving back to Minneapolis, Minnesota where he owned a successful saloon on the corner of 1st Street and 1st Avenue. Oscar Gardner died at age 56 on Christmas Day, December 25th, 1928 in Minneapolis, Minnesota, being inducted into the Minnesota Boxing Hall of Fame. He is considered one of the greatest featherweights of his era.

References:
http://www.mnbhof.org/Minnesota_Boxing_Hall_of_Fame/Oscar_Gardner.html
The New York Times
The Reading Eagle
The Evening Telegraph

GEORGE GARDNER

George Gardner, the Celtic Warrior, was the Light Heavyweight Champion of the World and an internationally famous fighter. He was the first Irish – American to win the World Light Heavyweight Title and he was one of the biggest names in boxing history. Gardner was once rated as the number one fighter in the world and he was a legend of the ring.

"Gardner is a great fighter. Many believe George Gardner is the best man in the world at 165 pounds. Experts who have seen him put up his hands have pronounced him a pugilist of merit with a brilliant future. If Gardner put on 20 pounds he could whip any fighter in the world." – Billy Madden, the boxer who coined the term "knockout", January 21st, 1903, *The Sun*

Sadly, he is most notable as the young 26-year-old champion who knocked out Jack Root for the title, and then lost his title to 40-year-old Bob Fitzsimmons after 20 rounds on points by decision.

George Patrick Gardner was born true "Fighting Irish" on St. Patrick's Day, March 17th, 1877 in Lisdoonvarna, County Clare, Ireland. His father was Michael Gardner, a prize – fighter, the son of Patrick Gardner, and the family immigrated in 1891 to America when George was 12 years old. The Gardner family landed in New York City and settled in Lowell, Massachusetts, near Boston.

He stood approximately 5' 11 ¾ tall, weighed anywhere from 150 to 175 pounds during his career, and had a workman like style. He was a clever in – fighter, ducked and moved well, fought at a good pace, he was a good puncher, very aggressive moving forward with his head down, and an excellent chin. Gardner had dark hair, a fair complexion, blue eyes, slightly muscular, and was one of the most talented and toughest fighters of his era.

His younger brother, Billy Gardner, 48 – 8 – 18 (26 KO's), was the Featherweight Champion of New England, standing 5' 8 ½ tall, weighing anywhere from 122 to 147 pounds, he retired in 1901 and he later removed to Pawtucket, Rhode Island.

His brother, Jimmy Gardner, 61 – 9 – 21 (39 KO's), was the Welterweight Champion of the World claimant from November 7th, 1908, to November 26th, 1908, defeating Jimmy Clabby and then drawing with him in New Orleans, Louisiana. He was 5' 7 ¾ tall and weighed anywhere from 133 to 153 pounds; the number one contender in the lightweight and welterweight divisions during his career. Gardner was one of the greatest Irish – American fighters of his era.

On November 5th, 1897, George Gardner defeated Hugh Colgren on points after 4 rounds in Manchester, New Hampshire in his professional debut. Then on his 21st birthday, he knocked out J. Young for the second time after two rounds in a rematch in Manchester, New Hampshire. Gardner had a string of eight knockout victories that year, including a first round KO of Tom O' Brien and a rematch against Hugh Colgren which resulted in a 3 – Round KO victory.

Gardner knocked out the tough African – American fighter Ed "Thunderbolt" Smith, 39 – 12 – 5 (32 KO'S) in the seventh round in 1898 on Christmas Day in Montreal, Quebec, Canada.

Afterwards, George Gardner, 10 – 0 (8 KO's) in 1899, fought a draw with Bob Montgomery and later knocked out the likes of Andy Moynahan, John Butler, and Young Sharkey. On July 31st, 1899 at Associate Hall in Lowell, Massachusetts, he buried Dick Sims in his own blood and after the crowd shouted, "Stop the contest!", a local sergeant called it off and although Gardner won the fight, the referee declared the bout a draw because of police interference. On August 5th, 1899, the Irishman defeated experienced veteran Harry Fisher, 24 – 6 (15 KO's) by 17 – Round TKO in Brooklyn, New York.

The undefeated George Gardner, 14 – 0 – 2 (12 KO's), faced heavyweight contender Jimmy Handler, 17 – 7 – 4 (9 KO's) and received his first loss by TKO after a grueling 18 rounds on October 16th, 1899 in Brooklyn, New York. A newspaper stated: **"The battle was productive of plenty of slugging and little science, but it was a furious contest and the patrons of the Hercules Club in Brooklyn, where the bout was held, were unanimous in their declaration that it was the greatest fight they had ever seen."**

"The Lowell man went down, but with the assistance of the ropes he regained his footing. Handler was at him like a flash, and with another punch on the jaw dropped him again. Gardiner made a game effort to rise and was just doing so as the sponge splashed in the center of the ring."

Then, at 154 pounds, he defeated Jack Moffat by 8 – Round TKO causing him to retire due to a broken arm. The year 1900 was perhaps his best year, because he would remain undefeated and defeat the best middleweights in the world. Gardner began the 20th Century off right after he knocked out Harry Fisher, 25 – 7 (16 KO's) for the second time in 12 rounds.

On February 12th, 1900, Gardner knocked out Jimmy Handler after 3 rounds in a rematch in Brooklyn, New York, avenging his loss. He also defeated the talented colored middleweight contender George Byers twice that year. Afterwards, he knocked out the lanky Charlie Goff, and later that year he traveled to Great Britain.

He knocked out the highly rated African – American fighter Frank Craig in 1900 in London, England, but other reports state he won by foul due to Craig being disqualified for throwing him. On September 30th, 1900, Gardner defeated British Heavyweight Champion Jack Scales by 3 – Round TKO victory. It was after this victory, he reunited with his family in Ireland, a celebration being held in his honor.

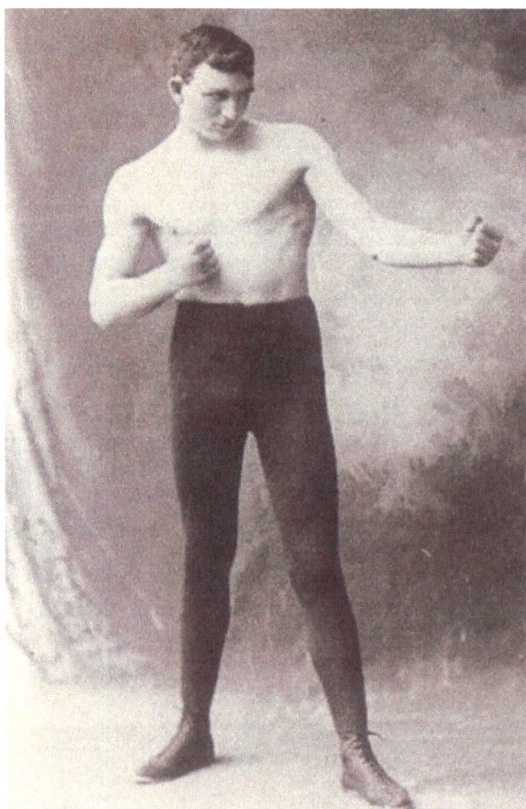

George Gardner, a feared fighter, now regarded as the Middleweight Champion of Great Britain according to newspapers, traveled to Cape Town, South Africa to face Lew Jones, but he failed to show. He arrived back in the United States and in 1901 he had his first title fight. Tommy Ryan was the reigning Middleweight Champion of the World according to record and although the Irish – American fighter was the number one middleweight contender in the world in 1901, Ryan refused to fight him when challenged.

However, it seems promoters and newspapers regarded George Gardner as the Middleweight Champion of the World.

On July 4th, 1901, George Gardner knocked out Jack Moffatt in a fight that was billed as the American and World Middleweight Championship titles at 158 pounds in San Francisco, California. Moffat was knocked down in the first round. Gardner finished him by 3 – Round TKO at the San Francisco Athletic Club.

He defeated Kid Carter by 18 – Round TKO on August 30th, 1901, at Mechanic's Pavilion in San Francisco, California in a fight that was advertised as the Middleweight Championship of the World.

However, in his next fight, he lost a decision on points to the talented welterweight "Barbados" Joe Walcott after 20 rounds in San Francisco, California.

On December 20th, 1901, George Gardner defeated Kid Carter by 8 – Round KO in San Francisco, California in a fight that was billed as the Middleweight Championship of the World. *Los Angeles Times* reported that the Irish – American fighter **"secured the World Middleweight Title"**. It seems George Gardner was the reigning World's Middleweight Champion in the eyes of the people instead of Tommy Ryan.

Then in January of 1902, he faced the popular and undefeated Jack Root in San Francisco and lost to him on a foul after 7 rounds.

On April 25th, 1902, George Gardner fought a rematch against 5' 1, 145 pound "Barbados" Joe Walcott, who was now the first African – American Welterweight Champion of the World. The six foot Gardner "trounced" the five foot Walcott. After 20 rounds, Gardner won by decision in San Francisco, California.

He was described as a **"whirlwind at in – fighting"**, according to his manager, Alec Greggains. He was confident that Gardner could **"trim any man in the country"**, including World Heavyweight Champion Jim Jeffries. Greggains stated in an interview:

"The boy is 100 per cent faster than he was when he last fought Root and showed it when he defeated Walcott. He has learned a lot, is like a kid to handle and will trim any man around his weight in this country. If Jeffries claims he can put him out in ten rounds I can get the money to back my man. The chief fault of the lad is to lose his head and go in like a bull, whereby he is apt to lose all gained on a foul."

On August 18th, 1902, George Gardner, 31 – 3 – 4 (25 KO's) knocked out undefeated Jack Root, 40 – 0 – 1 (27 KO's) after 17 rounds in front of a crowd of Arizona miners in Salt Lake City, Utah. The fighters both weighed in at 165 pounds and the fight was billed as the Middleweight Championship of the World. Root's corner threw in the sponge before he was counted out, resulting in a 17 – Round TKO, and newspapers reported that Gardner killed Root in the fight.

George Gardner was the first man to knock out and defeat Jack Root. He was then set to face Joe Choynski, the talented Jewish fighter, in Los Angeles, California, but the fight was cancelled. Instead, he faced the "Galveston Giant", Jack Johnson, 8 – 3 – 6 (7 KO's), who would later be classed as one of the greatest of all – time.

On October 31st, 1902, George Gardner, 32 – 3 – 2 (26 KO's), fought Jack Johnson, the future first African – American Heavyweight Champion of the World, and proved himself as a scrappy and game fighter. Although Johnson weighed in thirty pounds heavier at 185 pounds and Gardner weighed in at 155 pounds, Gardner floored Jack Johnson in the first round, and the "Galveston Giant" was only able to knock the clever Irishman down in the 8th and 14th rounds. Despite, the weight advantage, Johnson failed to knockout the Irishman, but the "Galveston Giant" won by close decision after 20 rounds on points in San Francisco, California. It is said Jack Johnson claimed George Gardner hit harder than anyone he had ever fought.

Gardner, now at 170 pounds, was classed in a new weight division and he was a top light – heavyweight contender. Lou Houseman, a boxing promoter and manager, had a fighter who was too big for the middleweight division at 160 pounds and to light for the heavyweights, so he created the Light – Heavyweight division in 1903 at 175 pounds. His fighter was none other than Jack Root, the first Light Heavyweight Champion of the World. After Root defeated Kid McCoy for the World Light – Heavyweight Title, he was the number one fighter in the world, pound – for – pound, and his only loss was to George Gardner.

The clever Irishman defeated Al Weinig, 23 – 13 – 3 (18 KO's) by 6 – Round TKO at the Maverick Athletic Club in Boston, Massachusetts and began his rise as a contender in the Light – Heavyweight division.

On April 6th, 1903, George Gardner knocked out Peter Maher in the first round at the Monarch Athletic Club in Boston, Massachusetts, a newspaper reporting that Maher **"stayed down more than the called for interval"**.

Peter Maher, the Irish Heavyweight Champion, was the most dangerous striker of his era. He was a famous fighter with a concussive knockout punch in both hands. Maher was the only Irishman to hold claim to the Heavyweight Championship of the World and still holds the record of the most knockout victories in boxing, with 50 first round knockout victories.

George Gardner, 35 – 4 – 2 (27 KO's), defeated Peter Maher, 124 – 11 – 4 (115 KO's), a veteran of over 100 fights, making him his 28th knockout victory.

On April 7th, 1903, *The Pittsburgh Press* reported:

PETER MAHER KNOCKED OUT IN THE FIRST ROUND

"Lowell, Mass. April 7 – Peter Maher, the Irish champion, went down to a quick defeat last night at the hands of George Gardner, of this city. The men were to have boxed 15 rounds, but Gardner put it all over Maher at the opening round knocked him out with a right to the jaw."

Then on May 13th, 1903, he defeated the "Fighting Kentuckian", Marvin Hart, 19 – 2 (16 KO's) by 12 – Round TKO in his hometown of Louisville, Kentucky at the Southern Athletic Club in a fight that was billed as the American and World Light – Heavyweight Titles. Gardner weighed in at 168 pounds and Hart weighed in at 176 pounds. Marvin Hart would later become the Heavyweight Champion of the World during his career.

George Gardner was now the No. 1 Light – Heavyweight contender in the world and challenged Jack Root for his title. *The Reading Eagle* reported that the champion would receive $7, 500 purse, a diamond medal, and that it would be the cleverness of Root versus the great ability of Gardner. Jack Root sported a record of 43 wins, 27 by knockout, 1 loss, and 1 draw; George Gardner sported a record of 37 wins, 29 by knockout, 4 losses, 4 draws, and 1 no contest.

The fight began at 3 o' clock. It was said Gardner weighed 165 pounds and gained three pounds in order to make weight. He weighed in at 168 pounds. Both men were noted for being in great shape. The fight was scheduled for 20 rounds in Fort Erie, Ontario, Canada. Gardner wore a green sash.

George Gardner, 5' 11 (reports vary from 5' 11 to 5' 11 ½ to 5' 11 ¾), 168 pounds, 37 – 4 – 4 – 1 (29 KO's), fighting out of Lowell, Massachusetts by way of Ireland, stood across the ring from Jack Root, 5' 10, 168 pounds, 43 – 1 – 1 (27 KO's), fighting out of Chicago, Illinois by way of the Czech Republic, reportedly the first World Light Heavyweight Champion.

On July 4th, 1903, George Gardner knocked out Jack Root by 12 – Round KO at the International Athletic Club in Fort Erie, Ontario, Canada for the Light Heavyweight Championship of the World. Gardner knocked Root down three times in the final round, counting him out after a vicious combination at 2: 20, the referee being Eddie McBride. The fight was one of the first caught on film, George Gardner being the second man in history to hold the title and the first Irish – American to hold the title.

Gardner was rated as the number one fighter in the world, pound – for – pound, and at age 26 he was on top of his game.

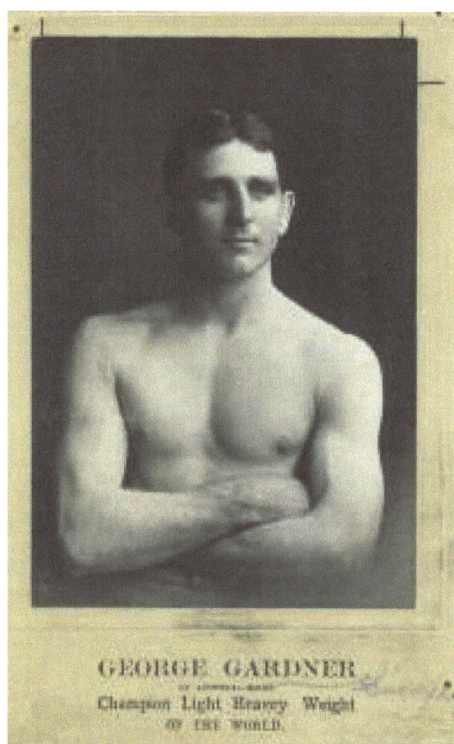

GEORGE GARDNER
Champion Light Heavy Weight
of the World.

On July 5th, 1903, *The Atlanta Constitution* reported:

GARDNER'S STIFF PUNCH PUT JACK ROOT TO SLEEP

On July 19th, 1903, *Spokesman Review* reported:

GARDNER A GREAT FIGHTER
DEFEAT OF ROOT MAKES HIM CHAMPION
"George Gardner, by his clean defeat of Jack Root, July 4, now stands out by himself in the light heavyweight division. He has as firm a hold on the title as Jeffries in the division above. He is undoubtedly a remarkable fighter, with more cleverness than he was credited with having. As a hitter he is a marvel and can stand all kinds of punishment without showing the white flag."

He held the title for four months, twenty – one days, from July 4th, 1903 to November 25th, 1903, George Gardner reigned as champion.

On November 25th, 1903, he lost his title in his first defense to old Bob Fitzsimmons after 20 rounds on points by decision. It made the young champion a footnote in history and it made Fitzsimmons even more of a legend. "Sunny Bob" Fitzsimmons became the first triple division title holder in the history of boxing, being the World's Middleweight, Heavyweight, and Light Heavyweight Champion.

The San Francisco Chronicle reported that Fitzsimmons floored George in the 4th, 5th, 13th, and 14th rounds. However, the *New York Times* reported that Gardner was never in any danger of being knocked out and was knocked down twice. It was considered one of the most boring title fights of its time with a small crowd.

"Gardner is a tough nut to crack. My hands were gone and I could do nothing. It dawned on me I would have to fight for a decision." – Bob Fitzsimmons

On November 26th, 1903, *Warsaw Daily Times* reported:
"The fight did not please the spectators, and the men in the ring were frequently hissed when they went through a round without apparently trying to fight. Referee Eddie Graney said that it was the worst fight he ever saw. He was forced to give the decision to Fitzsimmons because the latter scored the knockdowns. It was apparent that neither man was qualified to claim championship honors."

However, George Gardner was still a top-rated light – heavyweight contender. He challenged Fitzsimmons to a rematch, but he refused. The old Fitz held his title only by avoiding fights until 1905 when he was defeated by "Philadelphia Jack O' Brien".

After losing his title, George Gardner, the former light heavyweight king, stepped back into the ring the next year in January of 1904 and fought a draw against Marvin Hart after 15 rounds in Boston, Massachusetts. He then fought two men on the same day. Gardner defeated Jim Driscoll and Fred Cooley on the same day on February 8th, 1904 both by 6 – Round Decision in Chicago, Illinois.

Although he proved he was still a viable fighter after the loss of his title, it seems Jack Root may have had the last laugh. The two fought a draw in February of that year, but in May of that year, Root won a 6 – Round Decision over him and almost had him out in the last round. It was the last time the mortal enemies fought each other.

Gardner defeated Root twice, both by knockout, one being for the world title. Root defeated Gardner twice, once by disqualification on a foul and once by decision. Both had drawn once with each other. And both held the World Light – Heavyweight Title. Although Jack Root was a notch above George Gardner in popularity, George Gardner was a notch above Jack Root in talent.

On August 15th, 1904, George Gardner knocked out Jim Jeffords cold after 3 rounds in Butte, Montana. Gardner stood about six foot and weighed 175 pounds while Jeffords was a giant at 6' 4, weighing over 200 pounds. He knocked Jeffords down three times and the last time, he put Jeffords away.

On Tuesday, August 16th, 1904, Page 4 of the *Deseret Evening News* reported:

JEFFORDS IS KNOCKED OUT.

Gardner Disposes of the Californian in Three Rounds.

"BUTTE, Mont., Aug. 15. – George Gardner tonight defeated Jim Jeffords in the third round, knocking him out with a right swing to the jaw that laid the flesh open and sent the Californian reeling and spinning to the floor. Jeffords struggled to his feet and gamely mixed it again with Gardner, who, with another swing, sent him to the floor again. Jeffords for the third time regained his feet, and in a dazed manner attempted to strike at Gardner, who calmly squared off, and landing again on his groggy opponent, walloped him one that dropped him like a log.

Jeffords lay like one dead for several moments, and was in his corner for about three minutes before he was able to comprehend anything.

Jeffords was no match against the Lowell man's cleverness, Gardner repeatedly jabbing his left and right into Jeffords' face. Jeffords would swing at Gardner with terrific force, though the blows almost invariably would go wild or be ducked by Gardner. With his long left, Gardner kept tantalizing Jeffords as if feeling him out, and when in the third the big fellow made an effort to get away from ripping lefts, Gardner swung his right to Jeffords' jaw with deadly effect, dazing and sending him to the floor."

Then in September of that year, he fought a 10 – Round Draw with heavyweight contender "Fireman" Jim Flynn in Denver, Colorado. The next year in 1905, Gardner held claim to the Heavyweight Championship of the World, as did others after Marvin Hart's controversial hold of the title, after becoming only the second man to defeat Jack Root. And it was that year that the Irish prize – fighter suffered his first knockout loss to Mike Schreck in Salt Lake City, Utah. Schreck was considered the first southpaw fighter on record and had George counted out for the first time in his career as he was beginning to rise in the final 20th round in a long, grueling battle.

On June 19th, 1905, George Gardner knocked out the hard-hitting Billy Stift after 5 rounds in Ogden, Utah and it was his last known victory in the ring. It was from 1906 to 1908 that he received a string of losses and draws to fighters such as Al Kaufman, Jim Flynn, and Terry Mustain. Although he lost to all three by knockout, none of them could knock out old George Gardner without a hell of a fight. It took Kaufman 14 rounds to have George out and it took Jim Flynn a good 18 rounds before the Irishman was down.

On May 18th, 1908, he lost to Tony Ross by 7 – Round TKO in Newcastle, Pennsylvania in his last recorded fight, a newspaper reporting: **"He was merely pretending weakness to get an opening"**. It was his worst performance during his fighting career and was better compared to most. No one ever was able to finish him in less than the seventh round, no one ever finished him in the early rounds, and no one ever finished him in his prime.

George Gardner retired with a record of 44 wins, 32 by knockout, 12 losses, 6 by knockout, 8 draws, 2 no contests, a total of 66 professional fights recorded.

However, his career as a prize – fighter continued when he was 36 years old, on Friday, January 24th, 1913, Page 2 of the *Grand Forks Herald* (Grand Forks, North Dakota) reported:

"George Gardner, Veteran Pugilist, Saves a Nice Nestegg; Still Fighting

Winona, Minn., Jan. 23. – George Gardner, a principal in more than 300 battles of the prize ring, a worthy opponent of some of the best fighters the gloved contests have produced, is in Winona. The battle – scarred veteran has been inside the ropes for 18 years and has fought before and drawn from their seats in applause more fight fans than any other light – heavyweight, it is declared.

Still Active in Ring.
Gardner is visiting friends here while on a trip west, incidentally talking fighting and through his manager is still picking some of the easy "velvet". His battles now are confined to the lesser lights although he says he is ready still to battle with any of them. While his career has pointed the way through scores of bloody fistic encounters and he has run the race of the average boxer, Gardner today said he would not concede that he had backed into the oblivion of the "wassers", and believes the ring still holds for him a few victories and the tingle of the money will hold him to the sport as long as he can secure fights and the crowds to watch the battles.

Gardner won the light – heavyweight championship from Jack Root in 12 rounds at Buffalo, N. Y., in 1903 in the prettiest fight the Buffalo fans remember. In an actual fight Gardner says the title was never taken from him. Bob Fitzsimmons, after his defeat by Jeffries, was Gardner's opponent Nov. 25, 1903 at San Francisco. Fitzsimmons was given the decision at the end of 20 rounds and both men stepped from the ring with broken hands. Eighteen months prior to that fight with Fitz, Gardner knocked out Kid McCoy at the Seaside Athletic club in 15 rounds. Gardner also fought and defeated Marvin Hart and the late Gus Ruhlin."

He was described as a **"tough aggressive fighter who could box but lacked a concussive punch and stamina was somewhat suspect"**, according to Matt Donnellon's book, _Peter Maher: The Irish Champion_. However, Gardner knocked out Maher in the first round. It seems George Gardner won most of his fights by knockout and no one ever finished him in his prime.

His brother, Jimmy Gardner named his son George Gardner, who later became a professional middleweight boxer.

After his career as a professional boxer had ended, he was a boxing promoter, referee, and saloon keeper. George Gardner owned a saloon in Chicago, Illinois and was also on the 1930 cover of "Self Defense Quarterly". He had married Margaret Smith in 1904 and the following year he fathered a son named Morgan Patrick Gardner who was born on March 14th, 1905 in Chicago, Illinois, fought as a light – heavyweight boxer, served as a Chicago police officer, dying on May 14th, 1979 in Chicago, Illinois.

Morgan Gardner, former light – heavyweight boxer, stood 6' 5, and was known as a tough cop on the streets of Chicago.

Morgan Gardner, George's son, was also a professional light – heavyweight boxer, standing 6' 5, weighing 200 pounds. However, he decided to choose a career in law enforcement. Gardner was a narcotics detective on the notorious Maxwell Street in Chicago, Illinois and was known as a tough character, often punching people out of windows, not taking anything from anyone.

Although Bob Fitzsimmons had proven himself as a formidable fighter at age 40, George Gardner proved himself as a formidable fighter at age 60 when he knocked out a gunman who was holding up his saloon at 914 Wilson Ave.

On Friday, December 24th, 1937, *Daily Times* (Chicago, Illinois) reported:

OLD RING CHAMP K. O.'s 'Tough Guy'

"Still wondering what hit him, Joseph Rainey, 35, 4536 Sheridan rd., is in Bridewell hospital today after an early Christmas escapade. Wandering into the saloon at 914 Wilson ave., Rainey became involved in an argument and pulled out a gun commanding the 30 customers to "line up." George Gardiner, 60, and snowy – haired, 6316 N. Glenwood ave., former light heavyweight champion, happened to be the owner of the place and he walked up to the intruder. Just as his bartender, Martin Connor, poised behind Rainey with uplifted club, Gardiner unhooked a left to the jaw that sent the stranger reeling. Connor brought down the club "just for good measure." Town Hall police said that Rainey will be charged with carrying a concealed weapon and disorderly conduct as soon as he is well enough to leave the hospital. Joe Rainey will tell you those old – timers really could and still can fight. He pulled a gun in the saloon owned by George Gardiner, who was light heavyweight champion in 1903, and look what happened."

George Gardner, the former Light – Heavyweight Champion of the World, died at age 77 on July 8th, 1954 in Chicago, Illinois. His tombstone reads, **"First Light – Heavyweight Champion of the World"**. On July 10th, 1954, *The New York Times* reported: **EX – RING CHAMPION DIES: George Gardner, 77, Won Light Heavyweight Title in 1903; Four former boxing champions will be among the pallbearers."** Boxing historian Mike Paul rated George Gardner as the #29 All – Time fighter in his rankings.

Courtesy to Laura Frank, great-granddaughter of George Gardner for information and boxing historian Dan Somrack for photographs

References:
Celtic Warfare: The Legend of the Gardner Brothers by Corey Gardner
Boxing in San Francisco by Daniel F. Somrack
Peter Maher: The Irish Champion by Matt Donnellon
Boxing Monthly: Bob Fitzsimmons vs. George Gardner, the day history was made by Gary Lucken

BILLY GARDNER

Billy Gardner, the Lowell Kid, was the Featherweight Champion of New England. He was a talented Irish – American fighter. Gardner was a gatekeeper in the featherweight division.

William Edward Gardner was born on August 23rd, 1879 or 1881 in Lisdoonvarna, County Clare, Ireland, the son of Irish prize – fighter Michael Gardner.

However, on the 1940 Census, he was living in Cumberland, Providence County, Rhode Island, his birthplace was listed as Northern Ireland.

Billy Gardner reportedly stood 5' 8 ½, weighing 135 pounds. On May 11th, 1896, 15 – year old Billy Gardner defeated Mike Connelly by 4 – Round KO in Manchester, New Hampshire. He went 18 – 0 until he lost a 6 – Round Decision to Andy Daly.

On February 12th, 1900, Billy Gardner defeated Lew Morgan by 1 – Round KO at the Hercules Athletic Club in Brooklyn, New York. The *Brooklyn Daily Eagle* reported: **"Three punches in twenty seconds brought this bout to a speedy conclusion. Morgan going to the floor twice and out."**

On November 11th, 1906, Gardner defeated Andy Daly by 11 – Round TKO in a rematch in Lawrence, Massachusetts. Then on December 11th, 1900, he defeated Jimmy Briggs, 28 – 1, by 12 – Round TKO in Boston, Massachusetts. On February 11th, 1901, Gardner defeated Patsy Haley, 24 – 18, by 14 – Round TKO.

On March 11th, 1901, Billy Gardner defeated Ben DeBerry by 8 – Round TKO for the Featherweight Championship of New England in Cambridge, Massachusetts. Afterwards, he went on to defeat the likes of Tommy Sullivan, Eddie Connolly, and Belfield Walcott. He even fought a draw with World Welterweight Champion Mike "Twin" Sullivan.

Billy Gardner retired with a record of 48 – 8 – 18 (26 KO's) and it is believed he had perhaps several other fights.

He married Mary Gallagher, they had five children named James H. Gardner, Mary Gardner, William V. Gardner, Jane Gardner, and George E. Gardner.

Billy Gardner died on February 23rd, 1950 in Rhode Island.

Gardner was described as **"a good fighter, who was scrappy, capable, and determined."** – Cyber Boxing Zone

Later in the 1950s in New York, a featherweight fighter named Billy Gardner was 10 – 0 (3 KO's) during his career.

References:
Celtic Warfare: The Legend of the Gardner Brothers by Corey Gardner

JIMMY GARDNER

Jimmy Gardner, the Irish Fighter, was the Welterweight Champion of the World, the number one lightweight contender, and the number one welterweight contender during his career. He and his brother George Gardner were the first brothers in history to win world titles. Gardner was considered one of the greatest Irish – American fighters of all time.

"Gardner was a scrappy competitor who knew how to fight." – Cyber Boxing Zone

James Francis Gardner was born on Christmas Day, December 25th, 1884 in Lisdoonvarna, County Clare, Ireland, he stood 5' 7 ¾, weighing 133 to 153 pounds. He began his career with a 1 – Round KO over Jockey Brady. Gardner knocked out Jimmy Reilly, 22 – 14 – 11, by 2 – Round KO in November of 1902 in Rhode Island.

He defeated the likes of Patsy Sweeney, Belfield Walcott, Harry Lewis, and Jack O' Keefe during his career.

On August 4th, 1905, Jimmy Gardner defeated African – American fighter Rufe Turner by 11 – Round KO in San Francisco, California and then on August 25th, he defeated Buddy Ryan by 15 – Round TKO in Colma, California.

Gardner had 12 straight victories in 1907, and then he faced the first African – American World Welterweight Champion "Barbados" Walcott. On January 7th, 1908, Jimmy Gardner defeated Joe Walcott by 12 – Round Decision in Boston, Massachusetts. He was now the number one welterweight contender.

On April 22nd, 1908, he lost to Mike "Twin" Sullivan by 25 – Round Decision for the Welterweight Championship of the World as recognized by the State of California.

On November 7th, 1908, Jimmy Gardner defeated Jimmy Clabby by 15 – Round Decision for the Welterweight Championship of the World in New Orleans as recognized by the State of Louisiana and the two later fought a draw later that month for the title.

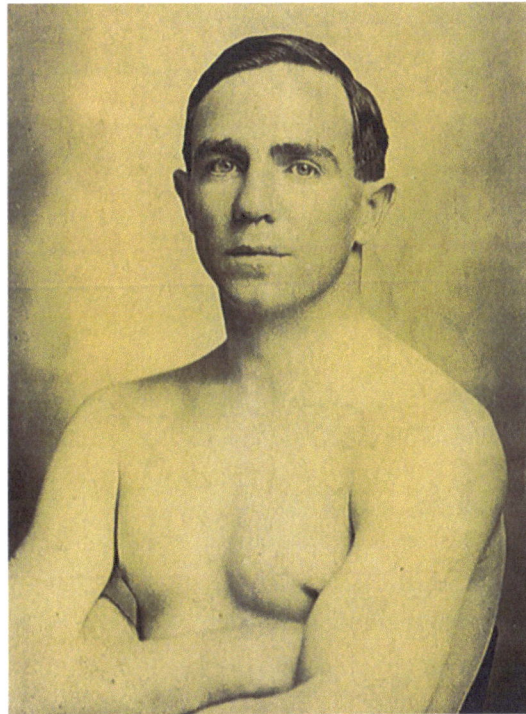

Gardner defeated Harry Mansfield, 14 – 6, by 1 – Round KO on January 25th, 1909 in Philadelphia. He then defeated Jack Fitzgerald by 4 – Round TKO. Afterwards, he defeated Bill MacKinnon, 9 – 0, by 12 – Round Decision.

He then lost to Frank Klaus and Jack Dillon as his career began to fade.

On January 18th, 1911, Gardner defeated Terry Martin, 39 – 14, by 3 – Round TKO in Fall River, Massachusetts, then retired at 25 years old.

On June 15th, 1917, Jimmy Gardner defeated Johnny "Kid" Alberts, 26 – 16, by 12 – Round Decision in Boston, Massachusetts, retired at 31 years old as a professional boxer.

He lost only four fights in his first eight years in the ring and was knocked out only twice during his career, towards the end.

Jimmy Gardner retired with a known record of 62 – 8 – 21 (39 KO's), though he possibly had more fights.

He married Alice T. Mountaine in 1903 and they had three children named Mary Gardner, Claire Gardner, and George Michael Gardner in Lowell, Masschusetts.

His son, George Michael Gardner, was a professional middleweight boxer.

On the 1950 Census, Jimmy Gardner was a 66-year-old widower, working as a janitor in Boston, Suffolk County, Massachusetts.

Jimmy Gardner died in May of 1964 in Massachusetts.

Courtesy to Laura Frank, great-granddaughter of World Light Heavyweight Champion George Gardner, for information.

References:
www.cyberboxingzone.com
Boxing in San Francisco by Daniel F. Somrack

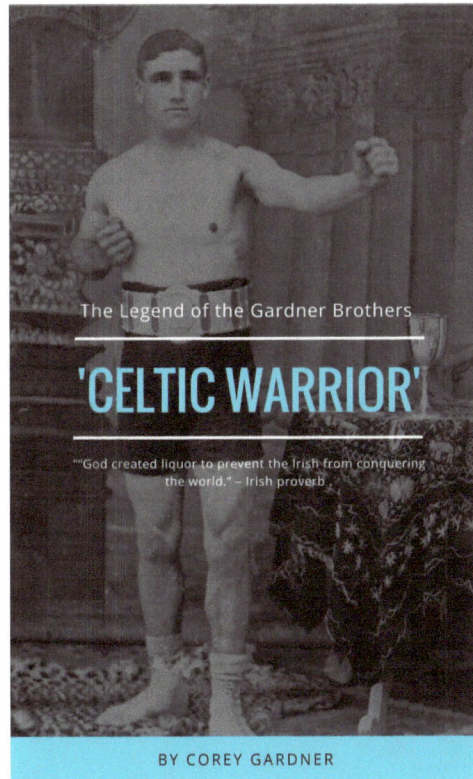

The Legend of the Gardner Brothers

'CELTIC WARRIOR'

"God created liquor to prevent the Irish from conquering the world." – Irish proverb

BY COREY GARDNER

"If there ever were three brothers who embodied Celtic warfare, it was the Gardner brothers of Lisdoonvarna, County Clare, Ireland.

George Gardner and Jimmy Gardner were the first Irish – American brothers to hold world championship titles. It was the Gardner brothers who give true meaning to the term, "Fighting Irish". They were the sons of an Irish prize – fighter named Michael Gardner who immigrated to the United States, settling in Lowell, Massachusetts.

On July 4th, 1903, George Gardner defeated Bohemian – American fighter Janos Ruthaly, better known as Jack Root, by 12 – Round KO for the World Light Heavyweight Title.

On March 11th, 1901, Billy Gardner defeated Ben DeBerry by 8 – Round TKO for the Featherweight Championship of New England in Cambridge, Massachusetts.

On November 7th, 1908, Jimmy Gardner defeated Jimmy Clabby by 15 – Round Decision for the Welterweight Championship of the World as recognized by Louisiana state in New Orleans. The two later fought a draw later that month for the title." – *Celtic Warfare: The Legend of the Gardner Brothers* by Corey Gardner

According to a family story, George, Billy, and Jimmy had a sister named Jenny Gardner who was married to middleweight fighter Joe Thomas. She trained as a boxer and while at a party, a female wrestler challenged her, telling her that a wrestler could beat a boxer. Jenny Gardner punched the female wrestler in the face once, knocking her out.

Michael Gardner (c. 1840 – 1916) married Bridget Morgan (1853 – 1924) on May 12th, 1869, they immigrated on April 18th, 1891 from Cloughane, Lisdoonvarna, County Clare, Ireland to America, settling in Lowell, Massachsuetts. They had eleven children. Their five sons were:

Patrick Morgan Gardner (1870 – 1927) New York Central railway police officer and veteran of both the Spanish-American War as well as World War I, died in an accident in Syracuse, New York.

George Patrick Gardner (1877 – 1954) World Light-Heavyweight Champion

William Edward "Billy" Gardner (1879 – 1950) New England Featherweight Champion

James Francis "Jimmy" Gardner (1884 – 1964) World Weltweight Champion

Michael Gardner (1889 – 1923) salesman, died from illness in Pennsylvania.

Patrick Morgan Gardner, the oldest son of Patrick and Bridget (Morgan) Gardner

Patrick Gardner, grandfather of the boxing Gardner family, had sons named James Gardner, Michael Gardner, and Peter Gardner (witnessed the wedding of Bridget Morgan and Michael Gardner).

John Gardiner, Ballinalacken, remembers: **"On a pleasant June afternoon in 1990 I had the pleasure of meeting John Gardiner (born 1892) near Ballinalacken Castle. John's father James (Seamas Paddy óg) was a brother of Michael Gardiner who married Bridget Morgan, my grandfather Michael's sister. They reared a family and lived above in Poll nag Con. Biddy (Bridget) as he recalled was the most charitable woman that ever lived. No one ever called to the door went away hungry. When the family were grown up they went to the States. Michael and Bridget had four sons, George, Paddy, Billy and Jimmy."**

"George, Billy, and Jimmy were boxers, trained in the States. George fought two fights in London and won them. When he came home they lit a fire for him (John remembers it) on top of a very exposed hill. George the Boxer could sit on a chair and let his hands hang down and his fingers would touch the floor."

John Gardiner mentioned a relative named Tomas Mór Gardiner.

Special thanks to Laura Frank, great-granddaughter of George Gardner.

References:
Morgan Family History

TOMMY GARDNER

Tommy Gardner, the Pacific Coast Terror, was the Bantamweight Champion of the Pacific Coast and the Northwest, regarded as one of the greatest fighters to come out of Walla Walla, Washington. He moved well and had fast hands. Gardner was a prospect in the bantamweight division.

"He was so fast, most of his opponents couldn't touch him. His reach was 42 inches, or more, and he had these round shoulders. And he was fast. He patterned himself after Gene Tunney. A very scientific fighter. And he named me after him." – Betty Gene Gardner

He was born in 1907 and began his boxing career at age 16 in June of 1923, losing by knockout in the first round, but he made a comeback, putting together six straight knockout victories, including a first round KO victory.

Gardner stood 5' 5 and weighed 118 pounds, a bantamweight fighter, who operated a barber shop on the side. After losing by 2 – Round KO to Vincent Hayes, Tommy Gardner went on a winning streak. He put together 23 straight victories in a row, including a decision victory over Vincent Hayes.

On March 22nd, 1929, Tommy Gardner won a diamond studded gold belt when he defeated Tommy Thank, 13 – 3, by 6 – Round Decision for the Northwest Bantamweight Title.

Gardner defeated Harvey Holliday, 20 – 8 – 5, by 6 – Round Decision on April 5th, 1929, at the Auditorium Theater in Spokane, Washington.

On October 8th, 1929, Gardner defeated Jackie Caston, 24 – 1, by 6 – Round Decision for the Pacific Coast Bantamweight Title in Seattle, Washington. *Everett Daily Herald* reported: **"Caston displayed plenty of nerve. Time after time he rushed in on his foe who stood a head taller and whose reach bested his by several inches. Gardner, the boxer, waited for Jacky, the fighter, to come in milling. He never had long to wait. A right to the head sent Caston to the canvas in the second round."**

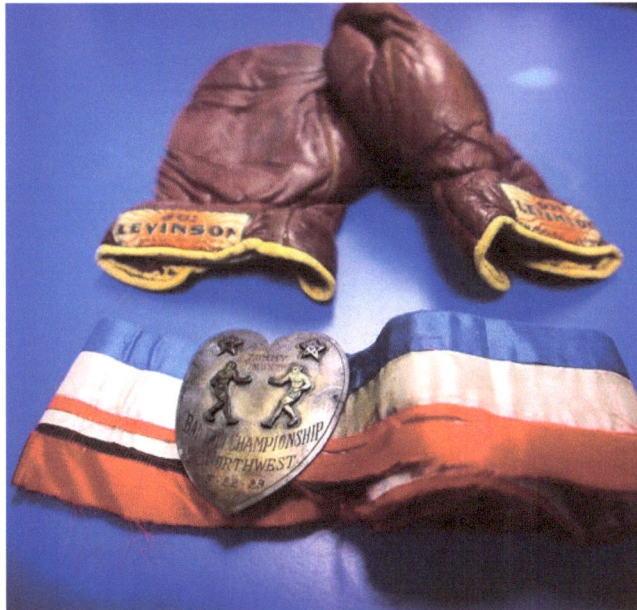

Tommy Gardner's Northwest Bantamweight Championship Belt

Tommy Gardner and his father, Harley, moved to Hollywood, California in 1930 for better competition. He won seven fights in a row before he lost a 10 – Round Decision to Newsboy Brown, and then he defeated Sergio Radam, 19 – 5 in August of 1930, his last fight. Tommy Gardner contracted polio that year and retired with a record of 35 – 4 – 2 (8 KO's).

He moved back to Walla Walla, Washington and opened "Tommy's Dutch Lunch". His daughter stated: **"And everybody came to see Daddy because he was a fighter. When he came in, that's when it was really popular."** Gardner was a crack shot when hunting and an avid skier. He divorced and remarried. Later, he died at age 74 in 1981, "more famous for his French fries than his fancy footwork."

Courtesy to Jim Buchan of the *Union Bulletin*.

References:
www.unionbulletin.com
Union Bulletin

TEDDY GARDNER

(Lord Lonsdale Belt; Public Domain)

Teddy Gardner, the Hartlepool Kid, was the Flyweight Champion of Great Britain, the British Empire, and Europe, a top ten contender for the Flyweight Championship of the World. He was a contender for the British Bantamweight Title. Gardner was one of the greatest fighters in the flyweight division.

He was rated as the #7 Flyweight in 1950; the #3 Flyweight in 1951; and the #6 Flyweight in 1952 according to *Ring Magazine.*

Edward Gardner was born on January 27th, 1922 and lived in West Hartlepool, County Durham, England.

On May 23rd, 1938, he began his boxing career at age 16 with a 4 – Round KO victory over Jack Herbert. However, in July of that year he lost his first fight against veteran Kid Rich, 7 – 16, by 10 – Round Decision. After a couple of victories, he lost another fight by 7 – Round TKO, but bounced back with a winning streak.

He put together 23 straight wins with 2 draws for the next eight years in an on and off career. He retired in 1940, but made a comeback in 1943 and even traveled to Bangalore, India. Gardner returned to England and lost to Gus Foran, 41 – 16, by 10 – Round Decision.

He defeated veterans Eddie Lewis, 41 – 6; Norman Lewis, 80 – 22; and Stan Rowan, 44 – 6; earning a title shot.

On December 13th, 1949, Teddy Gardner fought Danny O' Sullivan, 26 – 3, for the Bantamweight Championship of Great Britain at Royal Albert Hall in London, England, losing by 9 – Round TKO due to a cut eye.

Afterwards, he lost to Fernando Gagnon, 63 – 13, by 4 – Round TKO in a title eliminator, and he then went on a 17 – fight winning streak against the likes of Dickie O' Sullivan, 20 – 11, and Vic Herman, 28 – 8, as a flyweight.

On February 8th, 1952, Teddy Gardner, 51 – 7 – 3 (11 KO's), defeated 5' 2 French Flyweight Champion and European Flyweight Champion, Louis Skena, 34 – 8 – 4, by 6 – Round KO for the Flyweight Championship of Europe in Newcastle, England.

Gardner was 30 years old and in his prime.

On March 17th, 1952, Teddy Gardner, 52 – 7 – 3 (12 KO's), defeated former World Flyweight Champion Terry Allen, 58 – 8 – 1, by 15 – Round Decision for the British and British Empire Flyweight Title, and the (EBU) European Flyweight Title in Newcastle, England.

Teddy Gardner, 53 – 7 – 3 (12 KO's), was the British, Commonwealth, and European Flyweight Champion.

On June 30th, 1952, he defended his European (EBU) Flyweight Title against Otello Belardinelli, 20 – 21 – 10, by 15 – Round Decision.

However, on September 8th, 1952, he lost his Commonwealth (British Empire) Flyweight Title to Jake Tuli, 10 – 0, by 12 – Round TKO in Newcastle, England.

Teddy Gardner retired with a record of 55 – 8 – 3 (12 KO's), 66 professional fights. He ran a pub and was a Hartlepool legend. The former British and European flyweight champion died at age 55 in 1977 in England.

References:
www.boxrec.com
Boxing News

JACK GARDNER

Jack Gardner, the "Fighting Guardsman", was the Heavyweight Champion of Great Britain, the British Empire, and Europe, as well as a top ten contender for the Heavyweight Championship of the World. He was tall, dark, and handsome with knockout power. Gardner was one of the hardest punchers in the history of the heavyweight division and one of the greatest fighters out of the United Kingdom.

"Boxing is a manly sport. Every boy should have to take part in it to some extent. It knocks the bully out of him and makes him respect the other fellow." – Jack Gardner

He was shy, quiet, and popular with the ladies. Gardner stood 6' 1 ½ with a 78 inch reach and weighed anywhere from 200 to 221 pounds during his career. He had black hair, brown eyes, dark – complexioned and looked more like a Spaniard than an Englishman. A newspaper described him as **"splendidly built with a creditable punch."** He was often described as **"film star handsome, with his impeccable taste for fine clothing, faultless hair and designer mustache."**

Gardner was a knockout artist with one shot KO power in both hands. He was a slow mover and lacked technique, but his strength and excellent chin made him a contender. The British described him as the greatest hope for the World Heavyweight Title. The Americans described him as the **"famous British killer"**. "The Fighting Guardsman" was a fan favorite of the era.

Jack Leonard Gardner was born on November 6th, 1926 in Market Harborough, England. He was raised on the family farm and his father, Len Gardner, a former boxer, was his first trainer. The Gardner brothers were all over six feet tall, powerfully – built, and had knockout power.

His brothers, Bob Gardner, 6 – 10 (6 KO's) and Rod Gardner 2 – 1 (2 KO's) were also professional heavyweight boxers. A family story tells of how Bob Gardner set a record at a local gym of knocking a man out in 13 seconds of the first round. However, his record was quickly beaten, when his brother, Rod Gardner knocked a man out in 12 seconds of the first round.

Jack Gardner served in the British Army during World War II in Germany, serving from 1945 to 1951, earning the rank of colour sergeant in the elite infantry unit known as the Grenadier Guards. He was fairly unpopular due to being a "skiver", often avoiding responsibilities and he was very anti – social. It was while as a guardsman, he began his amateur boxing career.

Gardner knocked out undefeated Peter Shepherd cold in the first round in the semi – finals for the London District Heavyweight Title. Shepherd awoke 8 hours later in a hospital. Afterwards, Gardner knocked out "Tiny" Joe Harding in the first round for the London District Heavyweight Championship.

He won the Army and Imperial Services Heavyweight Titles, making him the BAOR Heavyweight Champion and the I. S. B. A. Heavyweight Champion.

Gardner defeated Johnny Morkus by 1 – Round TKO for the British Amateur Boxing Association ABA Heavyweight Title in 1948, having defeated Frank Bell by disqualification in the quarterfinals. Gardner then competed in the Olympic Games held in London. It was the first time the Olympic Games were shown on television.

GARDNER - VOL. III

As an Olympic boxer, Jack Gardner knocked out Ken Wyatt in the first round. Then he knocked out the Austrian boxer Karl Ameisbichler in the second round. However, he was defeated in the quarterfinal on points to Hans Muller, of Switzerland.

"AMATEUR PERSONALITIES" No. 1
SGT. JACK GARDNER (Grenadier Guards)
"A.B.A. and I.S.B.A. Heavyweight Champion, although he has been boxing over four years, he suddenly sprang into prominence this year by defeating two well – known amateur heavyweights in Frank Bell (Birkenhead) and J. Morkus (London).

Knocked out K. Ameisbichler (Austria) in the Olympics then went down to H. Muller (Switzerland) on points. Splendidly built with a creditable punch, not yet 22, is considered an excellent prospect and has plenty of time to lift an Olympic title yet."

After the Olympic Games on October 1st, 1948, Gardner knocked out Danish boxer L. Petersen in the second round in Copenhagen, Denmark. Then on October 6th, 1948, Gardner defeated the Swedish boxer and Olympic Silver Medalist Gunnar Nilsson on points. Afterwards, he finished his amateur career.

On December 6th, 1948, Jack Gardner won three fights all by knockout in the first round on the same night, making his debut as a professional fighter. His manager was John Simpson and he was signed to compete in a professional heavyweight novice tournament, promoted by Jack Solomons. It took place at the Harringay Arena in London, England.

Gardner defeated Hugh O' Reilly by 1 – Round TKO, then Harry Bedford by 1 – Round TKO, and then Ron Raynor by 1 – Round KO, winning the prize money.

Jack Gardner was 13 – 0 (13 KO's) as a professional boxer, his first year in the ring, 7 knockouts in the first round.
On January 31st, 1949, he defeated Nick Fisher, 15 – 4 (11 KO's), by 5 – Round TKO due to a cut. Gardner defeated tough Matt Hardy, 16 – 21 (11 KO's), by 1 – Round KO. He then defeated Les Pam by 2 – Round TKO.

Gardner knocked out "KO" Gene Fowler, 13 – 25 (5 KO's) in the first round. Fowler, an African – American born in Brooklyn, New York, had been the Maritime Light Heavyweight Champion, as well as the reigning British Army and Canadian Light Heavyweight Champion for three years. On March 14th, 1949 at Town Hall in Northamptonshire, England, topping the bill, Fowler fell in first round to the punching power of Jack Gardner.

"The Fighting Guardsman" knocked out a game Johnny Morkus by 4 – Round TKO. Morkus was knocked down in the third round, but after he had risen, he knocked Jack's mouthpiece out. Gardner finished him against the ropes, the referee stopping the fight on March 29th, 1949 at Earls Court Empress Hall in London, England.

On April 11th, 1949, Gardner knocked out Bill Brennan, 4 – 11 (3 KO's), in the first round with body punches at Ice Rink in Nottingham, England.

On April 19th, 1949, Gardner defeated Tommy Brown, 7 – 6 (3 KO's) by first round knockout after 140 seconds including the count. Brown was down four times. The fight took place at the Embassy Rink in Birmingham, England.

On May 3rd, 1949, he faced 6' 3 heavyweight Frank Ronan, 20 – 8 (12 KO's) whom he defeated by 3 – Round TKO while he was out on the ropes at the Earls Court Empress Hall in London, England.

On June 13th, 1949, Gardner defeated Ken Shaw, the Scottish Heavyweight Champion, 23 – 9 (5 KO's) by 7 – Round TKO due to cuts at Granby Halls in Leicester, England.

On June 27th, 1949, Gardner defeated knockout artist Charlie Collett, 45 – 19 (33 KO's) by 2 – Round KO at Dolphin Greyhound Stadium in Berkshire, England.

Jack Gardner, 13 – 0 (13 KO's) had defeated all of the British heavyweights put in front of him. His next opponent was colored Canadian Heavyweight Champion, Vern Escoe, 19 – 11 (7 KO's). It was Gardner's first loss on the professional circuit, losing by 5 – Round TKO due to cuts.

Later that month in July of 1949, he defeated Frank Walker by 4 – Round TKO by corner stoppage and the Belgian fighter Prosper Beck by 2 – Round TKO due to an injury.

On July 21st, 1949, Jack Gardner defeated 6' 5 Swedish fighter Nils Andersson, 11 – 6 (6 KO's) by 5 – Round TKO. Gardner knocked the Scandinavian down in the 3rd round. Then in the 5th round, the Swede quit.

On October 11th, 1949, he defeated Belgian Heavyweight Champion Robert Eugene by 5 – Round TKO due to retirement.

He fought inside the distance in 18 professional fights. On October 31st, 1949, Jack Gardner, 17 – 1 (17 KO's) defeated French Heavyweight Champion Stephane Olek, 20 – 9 (16 KO's) by 8 – Round Decision, going the distance for the first time in his career at Granby Halls in Leicester, England.

On February 13th, 1950, "The Fighting Guardsman" suffered his second defeat to the same opponent. Vern Escoe, 22 – 11 (9 KO's), the colored Canadian Heavyweight Champion defeated the young English fighter by 8 – Round Decision on points. Although Escoe scored freely, he failed to land a knockout punch on the granite jaw of Gardner. It was in the fourth round, Gardner dropped Escoe twice and in the seventh he dropped the Canadian heavyweight champion with a big right hand, but still he lost the decision on points.

Jack Gardner, 18 – 2 (17 KO's), defeated Belgian Heavyweight Champion Robert Eugene by 3 – Round KO in a rematch in June of 1950 and despite two losses to the Canadian Heavyweight Champion, he was in line as a contender.

His next fight was for the British Heavyweight Title Eliminator.

On July 17th, 1950, Jack Gardner, 19 – 2 (18 KO's), defeated Johnny Williams, 41 – 3 – 2 (25 KO's) by 12 – Round Decision at Granby Halls, Leicester, England in the "Fight of the Year". Although Williams was the superior boxer, Gardner was the superior striker. The fight was dubbed the **"Bloodbath of the Midlands."**

After the fight, Williams passed out for 15 minutes, being sent to the hospital. Jack Gardner was now the No. 1 Contender for the Heavyweight Championship of Great Britain and the British Empire. He challenged Bruce Woodcock, the Heavyweight Champion of Great Britain and the British Empire, for his titles.

Bruce Woodcock, 35 – 3 (31 KO's), had went 20 – 0 (20 KO's) his first years in the ring. He was the most dominant fighter in the heavyweight division in Great Britain for 5 years, fighting out of Doncaster, England. Woodcock was a top ten contender for the World Heavyweight Title and he had successfully defended his titles, reigning as champion.

On November 14th, 1950, Jack Gardner, 20 – 2 (18 KO's) fought the popular British Heavyweight Champion Bruce Woodcock, 35 – 3 (31 KO's) for the Heavyweight Championship of Great Britain and the British Empire.

Jack Gardner defeated Bruce Woodcock by 11 – Round TKO due to retirement.

Woodcock, the #5 Contender for the World Heavyweight Title, lost sight in his eye as it began to close and the fight was stopped. It was the champ's last fight. Bruce Woodcock retired and wrote a book titled, _Two Fists and a Fortune_.

The British Army hosted a celebration dinner for the newly crowned champion which included a special visit from Princess Elizabeth.

Jack Gardner, 21 – 2 (19 KO's) was the Heavyweight Champion of Great Britain and the British Empire.

"BOXING NEWS" PHOTOS. No. 53

JACK GARDNER
BRITISH HEAVYWEIGHT CHAMPION

SUSSEX DAILY NEWS MARCH 19TH 1951

WED. at 3 p.m.

JACK GARDNER

British Empire Heavyweight Champion

WILL BE

HERE

49 NORTH ST. BRIGHTON

Telephone 28614
(OPPOSITE ESSOLDO)

BARRINGTONS

(TAILORS)   LIMITED

OVER 2000 GARMENTS READY-TO-WEAR !

SUITS	TROUSERS	JACKETS
In all Styles, Pinheads, Hopsacs, Serges, Gaberdines, Stripes, and Fancies.	27 Shades, 48 Fittings, Worsteds, Gaberdines, Hopsacs, Baratheas, and Twill Designs.	In all styles, Diagonals, Checks, Harris Tweeds, and Fancy Weaves.
from £5-9-0	from £1-12-6	from £2-8-9

AND GOOD SELECTION OF RAINWEAR

CHAMPIONS IN THE FIELD OF TAILORING !

(Courtesy to *The Argus* and Philip Bye of the Essex Record Office)

Jack Gardner, the Heavyweight Champion of Great Britain and the British Empire, was the #8 Contender for the Heavyweight Championship of the World in Ring Magazine Annual Ratings. He was even rated above undefeated American Rocky Marciano. Gardner was the #9 Heavyweight in the world.

February 1951 Ring Magazine 1950 Annual Ratings:
Joe Louis
Lee Savold
Joey Maxim
Clarence Henry
Bob Baker
Rex Layne
Jersey Joe Walcott
Jack Gardner
Lee Oma
Rocky Marciano

On March 27th, 1951, Jack Gardner defeated 6' 3 ½ Austrian fighter Jo Weidin, the European Heavyweight Champion, 28 – 7 (21 KO's) for the (EBU) European Boxing Union Heavyweight Title by 15 – Round Decision on points. The fight took place at Earls Court Empress Hall in London, England. It looked as if Gardner could finish the fight at any moment, knocking out Weidin's mouthpiece in the 14th Round and winning 11 rounds of the fight despite having a broken thumb.

Jack Gardner, the Heavyweight Champion of Great Britain, the British Empire, and Europe, #8 Contender for the World Heavyweight Title, #9 Heavyweight in the world, sported a record of 22 – 2 (19 KO's).

Gardner was the greatest British white hope for the World Heavyweight Title since the 19th Century.

On June 5th, 1951, he fought contender Cesar Silverio Brion, 30 – 5 (15 KO's) a New York based Argentine fighter in Marciano's training camp, who had defeated American contender Tami Mauriello by 2 – Round TKO. The fight took place at White City Stadium in London, England. The Associated Press gave Brion 5 rounds, Gardner 3 rounds, and 2 rounds even, Cesar Brion winning by 10 – Round Decision on points. Due to his close decision loss to Brion, he dropped from the top ten rankings as a contender for the World Heavyweight Title.

The Fighting Guardsman: The Fighting Career of Jack Gardner, a booklet by Evan R. Treharne, examined his boxing career and it was in the author's opinion that Jack Gardner had the potential to become the Heavyweight Champion of the World.

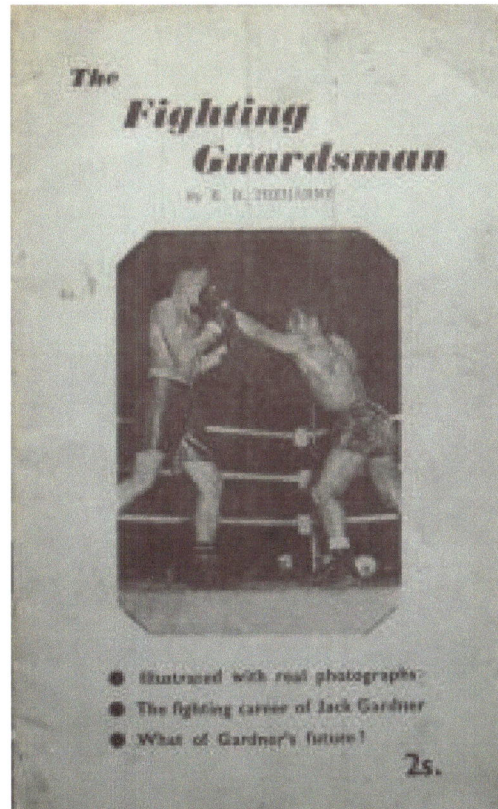

On September 23rd, 1951, Jack Gardner defended his European Heavyweight Title against the 6' 5, German Heavyweight Champion, Hein Ten Hoff, 21 – 1 (18 KO's), at Waldbuehne in Berlin, Germany. Ten Hoff had only lost one fight to that point, to World Heavyweight Champion Jersey Joe Walcott by decision. Gardner could not get past the reach advantage of Ten Hoff and lost his European Heavyweight Title by 15 – Round Unanimous Decision.

On March 11th, 1952, Jack Gardner, 22 – 4 (19 KO's), defended his British and Commonwealth (British Empire) Heavyweight Titles against #10 Contender Johnny Williams, 46 – 5 – 3 (29 KO's), in a rematch at Earls Court Empress Hall in London, England. It was the cleverness of Williams versus the power of Gardner. The Associated Press gave 6 rounds apiece to Gardner and Williams, 3 rounds even. It was one of the closest fights in British boxing history.

The ex – guardsman lost his British and British Empire Heavyweight Titles by controversial 15 – Round Decision. On March 12th, 1952, *The New York Times* reported: **"Johnny Williams Wins British Titles by Beating Gardner as Fans Boo Decision"**. The British press called for a rematch.

However, disgusted with the decision, he retired and bought a 62 – acre chicken farm with his winnings. As a family man, he worked odd jobs to provide for his wife and children. After working as a car salesman and lorry driver, he returned to his career as a prize – fighter.

BOXING NEWS, MARCH 5, 1952

TRIBUTE TO SYDNEY HULLS—Pages 8-11

A RINGSIDE SEAT AT EVERY FIGHT

BOXING NEWS

World's Premier Fight Weekly

VOL. 8 No. 10 43rd YEAR — Registered at the G.P.O. as a Newspaper. — PRICE SIXPENCE — MARCH 5, 1952

BATTLE OF BIG BOYS
GARDNER DEFENDS TITLES AGAINST WILLIAMS

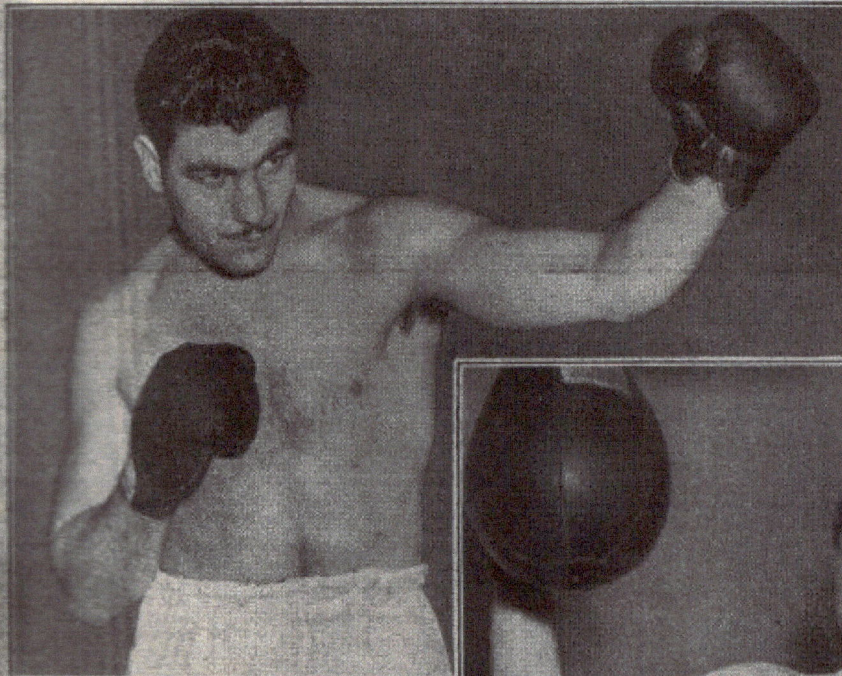

On the left:

JACK GARDNER
British and Empire Heavyweight Champion. Market Harborough. Born November 6, 1926.

Bouts	Won	Lost	Drawn	Winning %
26	22	4	0	84.62

On the right:

JOHNNY WILLIAMS
Barmouth. Born Dec. 25, 1926.

Bouts	Won	Lost	Drawn	Winning %
52	43	6	3	85.58

BIGGEST fight of the year, both in size and importance, takes place at the Exhibition Hall, Earls Court next Tuesday when Jack Gardner defends his British and Empire heavyweight titles against his outstanding challenger, Johnny Williams. They meet over fifteen rounds and if they produce a fight as gruelling and as thrilling as their previous encounter in 1950, then London fans are in for a treat.

A great deal depends on the outcome of this scrap and Jack Solomons has been in America during the past week making plans to match the winner with the leading heavies on the other side of the Atlantic. If Gardner wins he will have gained a second notch on the Lord Lonsdale Belt; if Williams is triumphant he will go after the World's title. The Editor sums up this important contest on page 2.

Jack Gardner, 22 – 5 (19 KO's), in December of 1953, made his comeback.

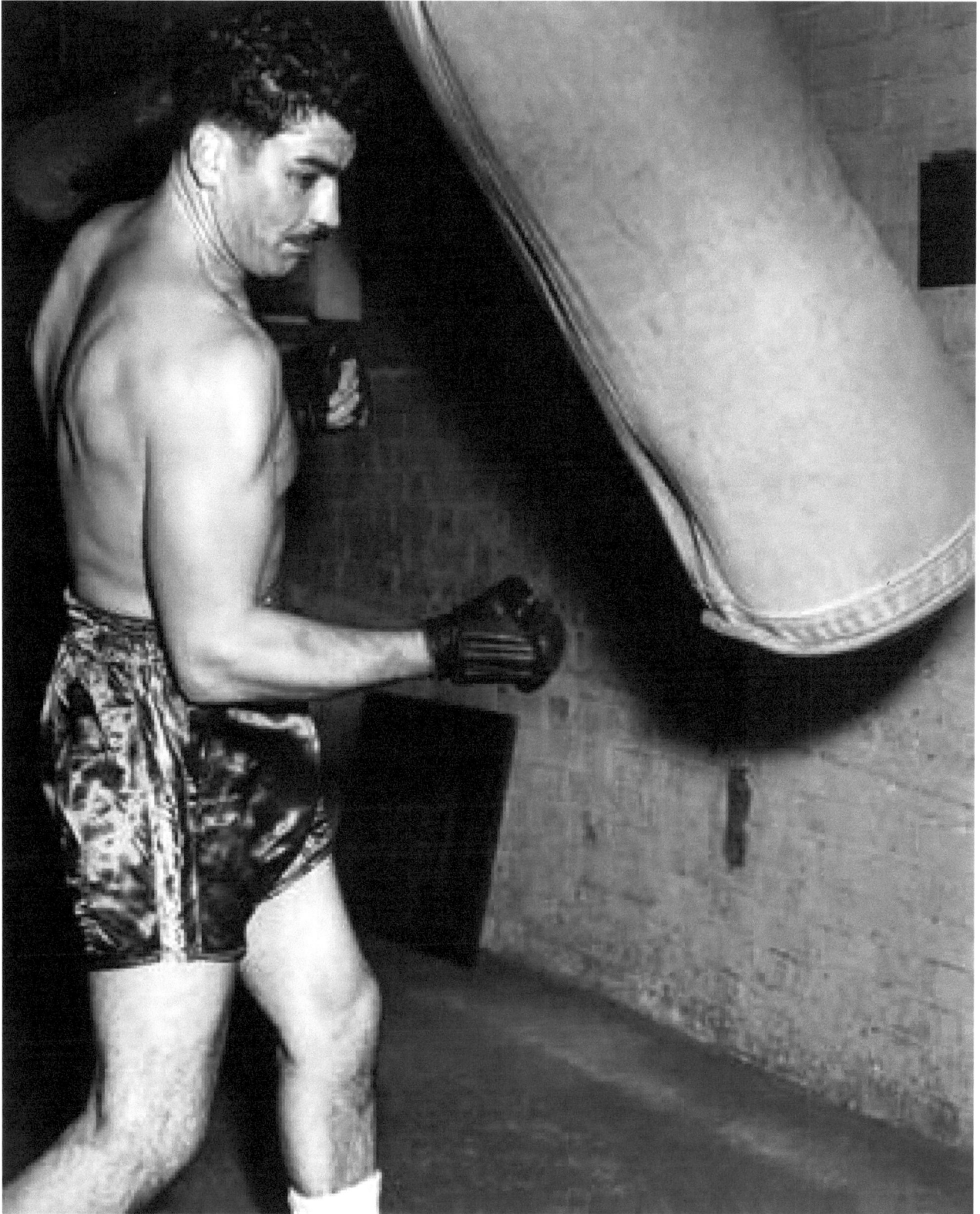

On December 8th, 1953, Jack Gardner defeated the Italian Heavyweight Champion, Uber Bacilieri, 11 – 4 – 5 (3 KO's) by 7 – Round TKO due to cuts at the Harringay Arena in London, England.

He then defeated Ansell Adams, 17 – 14 – 1 (8 KO's) by 10 – Round Decision and Frank Bell, 17 – 11 – 1 (11 KO's) by 6 – Round TKO in 1954 at Granby Halls in Leicester, England.

Gardner defeated French Heavyweight Champion, Lucien Touzard, 7 – 3 – 1 (5 KO's) by 4 – Round TKO due to a cut.

His next fight was for the British and Commonwealth Heavyweight Title Eliminator. His opponent was none other than his arch rival, Johnny Williams, the #6 Contender. The Welsh boxer was on an eight-fight winning streak.

On June 6th, 1955, Jack Gardner, 26 – 5 (22 KO's), fought Johnny Williams, 59 – 7 – 3 (37 KO's) in a rubber match. Jack Gardner vs. Johnny Williams III, the trilogy fight, was one of the biggest rivalries in British boxing history. It ended at Ice Stadium in Nottingham, England.

On June 7th, 1955, *The New York Times* reported:
"GARDNER WINS IN FIFTH; Knocks Out Williams to Earn Title Bout With Cockell."

Gardner knocking out Williams.

Although Williams was knocked out by Gardner, the Welshman was not out of his prime. It was in his next fight that Williams defeated up and coming contender, Kitione Lave by 1 – Round TKO. However, Williams suffered a string of losses afterwards, retiring after a 6 – Round TKO loss to Joe Bygraves.

Gardner had a record of 27 – 5 (23 KO's) and in 32 professional fights, he had never been knocked down during his career. He was the #1 Contender for the British Heavyweight Titles held by his sparring partner and former world title challenger, Don Cockell, 66 – 12 (33 KO's). However, due to an injury, the two British fighters had warm – up fights.

On December 13th, 1955, 29 – year old Jack Gardner defeated the "The Tongan Terror", South Pacific Heavyweight Champion, Kitione Lave, 26 – 5 – 2 (21 KO's) by 10 – Round Decision. Lave knocked Jack down for the first time in his career. The Englishman was down twice in the first round, and had a broken nose. Despite being knocked down for the first time in his career, Gardner beat the count and gained the decision. However, the British newspapers were in an uproar, believing Lave had won the decision.

After the controversial decision win at Embassy Sportsdrome in Birmingham, England, he had another warm – up fight.

On April 24th, 1956, Jack Gardner, 28 – 5 (23 KO's), fought Liverpool based Jamaican, Joe Bygraves, 30 – 8 (12 KO's) at Earls Court Arena in London, England. He lost by 2 – Round TKO due to cuts. *The Palm Beach Post* reported: **"Jack Gardner had a deep cut under right eye causing him to lose by TKO to Joe Bygraves in the second round."**

On the same fight card, Don Cockell was knocked out in the second round by Kitione Lave. It was a changing of the guard. The fight between Cockell and Gardner never happened, and Bygraves later became the British Empire Heavyweight Champion defeating Kitione Lave by 15 – Round Decision.

Jack Gardner retired at age 29 with a record of 28 – 6 (23 KO's). He owned a gym at Highfields in Leicester, England. Gardner also ran a pub which his parents had owned in Great Oxendon near Market Harborough, England.

"He was 13 – 0 (13 KO's), with 7 first round knockout victories as a prospect. He went 32 professional fights without being knocked down in the heavyweight division. He finished 23 of his 28 victories. His granite chin and deadly knockout power threatened the World Heavyweight Title. As one of the deadliest strikers, he conquered Great Britain, Europe, and the British Empire. Who was this British warrior? His name you ask? They called him the "Fighting Guardsman". I nicknamed him "Gentleman Jack". His name was the legendary Jack Gardner." – *Gentleman Jack: The Fighting Career of Jack Gardner* by Corey Gardner

Jack Gardner at Tiger Sports Stadium in Brighton

(Courtesy to Mrs. Trevor Chepstow)

On April 11th, 1972, the *Glasgow Herald* reported:
Boxing
Heavy – weight hope sought

"Jack Gardner, former British heavyweight champion, now a farmer, has joined forces with Johnny Griffin, the Midlands manager, to search for a heavyweight hope.

Gardner, who himself came to wealth and fame when he won a heavyweight competition, will look after the training of the boxer, and Griffin will do the managing."

Jack Gardner, quiet and charming, served his country, displayed his talent as a fighter becoming a champion, and retired quietly to his farm as a family man. On November 11th, 1978, he died at age 52 from a brain tumor while at a hospital, his body was cremated, his ashes being scattered under a Grenadier apple tree on his farm. "The Fighting Guardsman" was locally known as the "Gentle Giant", a sports hall was named after him, and there is a seat dedicated in his memory in the town square in Market Harborough, England, where he is still a legend.

References:
The Fighting Guardsman: The Career of Jack Gardner by Evan Treharne
Gentleman Jack: The Fighting Career of Jack Gardner by Corey Gardner

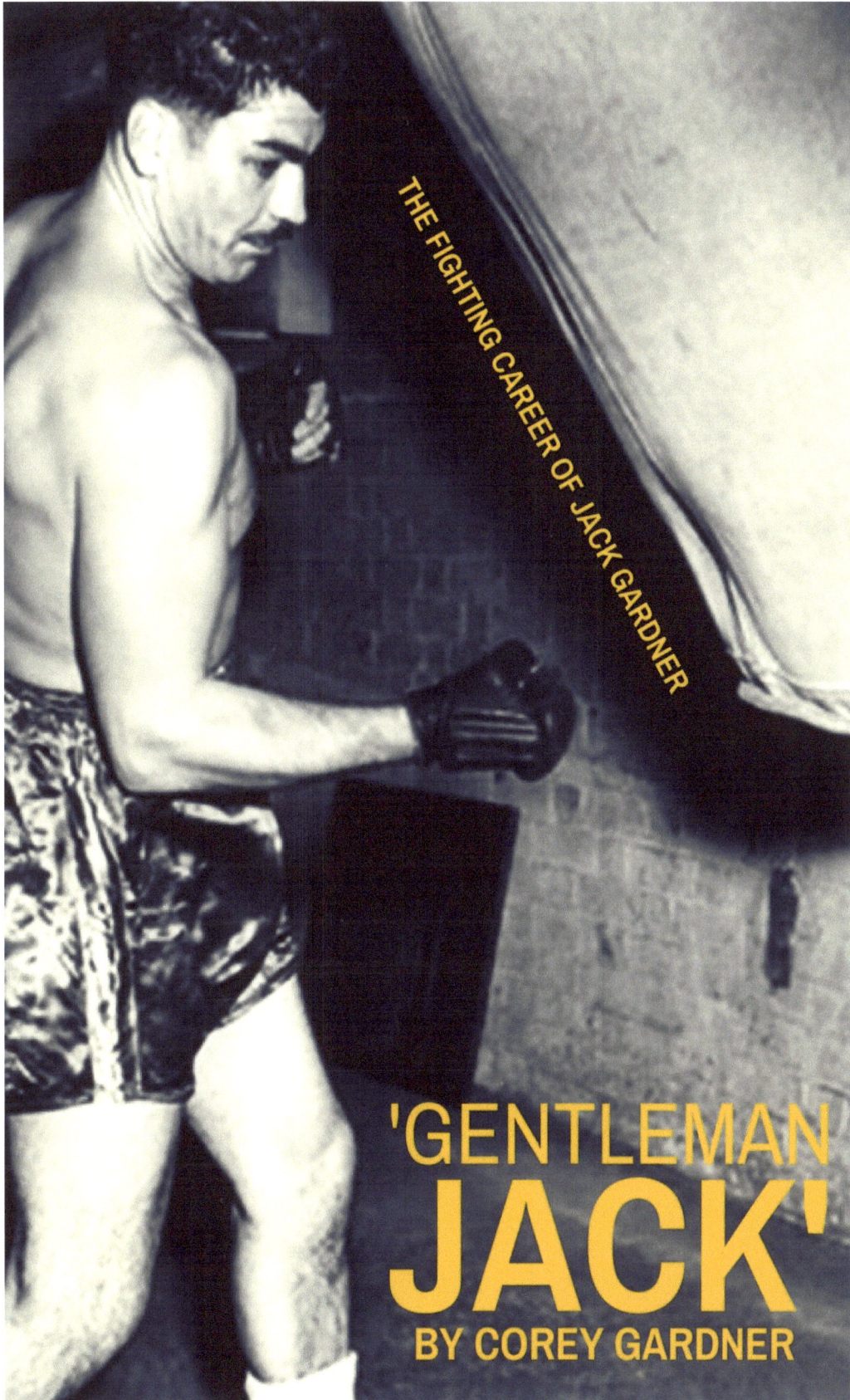

THE FIGHTING CAREER OF JACK GARDNER

'GENTLEMAN
JACK'
BY COREY GARDNER

TYRONE GARDNER

Tyrone Gardner, the "Tiger", was the Lightweight Champion of Canada, a legendary fighter in Cape Breton, Nova Scotia. He was a lightweight fighter with knockout power. Gardner won the Nova Scotia, Maritime, Eastern Canadian, and Canadian lightweight titles during his career.

Tyrone Gardiner was born on April 3rd, 1939, a native of Sydney, Nova Scotia, Canada. His father was Henry Gardiner and as a teenager Tyrone began his career as a professional fighter. He was only fifteen years old when he had his debut.

On September 6th, 1954, Tyrone "Tiger" Gardner defeated Wally Gillis by 2 – Round KO and then on January 1st, 1955 he defeated Kid Chaisson by 4 – Round Decision. After fighting a 4 – Round Draw against Leckie Mansfield later that month, in March of that year, Gardner defeated Leckie Mansfield by first round knockout. It was during this time he was training under Johnny Nemis in Cape Breton.

On December 4th, 1955, Gardner defeated Bobby Duff by 4 – Round Decision, making him 5 – 0 – 2, but in January of 1956, at age 16 he was defeated for the first time against Charley McIntyre by 4 – Round Decision. He then lost by 2 – Round KO to in a rematch against Bobby Duff in May of that year, along with a decision loss to Jackie MacPhee. However, he bounced back with a 2 – Round KO over Jack Sponagle in Stellarton, Nova Scotia, Canada.

After a loss and a draw, at age 17 he took two years off from November of 1956 to November of 1958 and made his comeback at age 19 with a 4 – Round Decision victory over undefeated Harold Tonnery. He then defeated Keith Gabriel by 6 – Round Decision, and took a year off again. It was in November of 1959 he lost to Tony Perry by 5 – Round KO and lost a rematch in April of 1960 by 6 – Round Decision.

It was during the summer of 1960 at age 21, he lost a 4 – Round Decision to Al Tonnery and his three-fight losing streak brought him to 9 – 8 – 3 (3 KO's) and now he had a new trainer named Johnny Cechetto.

On October 28th, 1960, Tyrone "Tiger" Gardner defeated Kenny Dean, 2 – 3, by 3 – Round KO and he went on a winning streak for one straight year. He defeated Sugar Ray Mascoll, 0 – 7 – 1 by 4 – Round Decision and on January 2nd, 1961, he defeated a novice named Young Hackey by 1 – Round KO beginning the year off right. It seemed at age 22, Gardner had reached his potential and was a contender among Canadian fighters.

Gardner knocked Bob McNeil down three times, winning by 4 – Round TKO at Venetian Gardens in Nova Scotia. He defeated George Munroe, 7 – 5 by 6 – Round Decision. On July 28th, 1961, Gardner knocked out Leroy Sparks, 5 – 4 in the first round and later he defeated Leroy Jones, 18 – 12 – 1, by 10 – Round Decision, along with Rejean Robert, 2 – 6, by 10 – Round Decision in September of that year.

On October 27th, 1961, Gardner defeated Jimmy Calhoun by 5 – Round KO and after his ninth straight victory of being undefeated for one year, he brought his record to 18 – 8 – 3 (8 KO's). On November 28th, 1961, Tyrone "Tiger" Gardner fought Les Sprague, 7 – 2, and lost a 6 – Round Decision. However, he put together five straight victories, four by knockout.

On January 2nd, 1962, Gardner knocked out Leo Steele, 4 – 2, in the first round, beginning the year off right once again. Then in April of that year he defeated Bobby Speight, 5 – 6 – 2, by 3 – Round KO and won a 10 – Round Unanimous Decision over Rollie Thibault. It was in July of that year he knocked out Bobby Speight again in the third round and later that month Gardner defeated Willie Weatherspoon by 3 – Round KO, earning his title shot.

On August 14th, 1962, Tyrone Gardner, 23 – 9 (12 KO's) at 136 pounds, fought Les Sprague, 10 – 3 (7 KO's) at 138 pounds, for the Canada Super Lightweight Title, but lost by 8 – Round TKO in Halifax, Nova Scotia.

On November 10th, 1962, Tyrone Gardner, 23 – 10 (12 KO's), fought former Canadian Lightweight Champion, Fernand Simard, 18 – 4 – 1 (8 KO's). Gardner defeated Simard by 6 – Round KO in Sydney, Nova Scotia, perhaps his greatest victory. Simard later became the Canada Super Lightweight Champion and the Canada Welterweight Champion during his career.

Tyrone "Tiger" Gardner, at age 24, earned his title shot again.

On May 18th, 1963, Tyrone Gardner, 24 – 11 – 3 (13 KO's), fought Les Sprague, 13 – 4 (9 KO's), for the Canada Super Lightweight Title, but lost by a close 12 – Round Split Decision.

On August 2nd, 1963, Gardner defeated Canada Super Featherweight Champion Buddy Daye, 16 – 7 (10 KO's), by 4 – Round TKO in Glace Bay, Nova Scotia, once again earning a title shot.

On October 26th, 1963, Tyrone Gardner, 26 – 11 – 3 (14 KO's) fought former Canada Bantamweight and Featherweight Champion Marcel Gendron, 12 – 5 (8 KO's) for the vacant Canada Lightweight Title. Gardner defeated Gendron by 4 – Round TKO victory. He was now a prospect in the lightweight division, possibly on his way to becoming a contender.

He traveled to Mechanics Hall, Worcester, Massachusetts in the United States to fight New England Welterweight Champion Dick French, 23 – 4 (8 KO's). On January 9th, 1964, he lost by 7 – Round TKO and later lost a 10 – Round Decision to Willie Williams, 13 – 4 – 2 (2 KO's) back in Nova Scotia. However, later that year he bounced back with a couple of victories.

On August 1st, 1964, Tyrone Gardner, 27 – 13 (15 KO's), fought hard hitting Fernand Chretien, 21 – 2 (12 KO's), who was on a ten-fight winning streak. Gardner defeated Chretien by 5 – Round TKO at Miners' Forum in Glace Bay, Nova Scotia. It was one of his best victories over a tough opponent.

Later in September of that year he defeated Leroy Jones, 19 – 4 (8 KO's) by 10 – Round Decision and afterwards the "Tiger" took a year off.

On September 6th, 1965, Tyrone "Tiger" Gardner, 28 – 13 (16 KO's) defeated Willie Williams in a rematch by 7 – Round KO in Glace Bay, Nova Scotia, and at age 26 he retired with a record of 29 – 13 (17 KO's).

Tyrone Gardiner was later inducted into the Nova Scotia Sports Hall of Fame.

TYRONE "TIGER" GARDINER

References:
Distinction Earned: Cape Breton's Boxing Legends 1946 – 1970 by Paul McDougall

Courtesy to the Nova Scotia Sports Hall of Fame for photographs, Katie Tanner, and Tyrone Gardiner

JOHN L. GARDNER

John L. Gardner, the "Hackney Rock", was the Heavyweight Champion of Great Britain, the Commonwealth, and Europe, one of the greatest fighters out of the United Kingdom. His toughness and aggression made him a contender. Gardner finished and defended all of his title fights during his career.

"Retiring professional fighters became a habit of mine." – John L. Gardner

"Boxing strips everything down to the bare bones, exposes all a man's strengths and weaknesses. You can end up being completely humiliated in the most public way imaginable, and I was never gonna let that happen to me – win or lose." – John L. Gardner

He stood 5' 11 and weighed around 205 pounds during his career. Although short and stocky for a heavyweight, his speed and aggression made him an action packed fighter. He had a good chin, great stamina, and excellent work ethic, but his lack of one punch power prevented him from being a fan favorite. Gardner finished most of his opponents by wearing them down and he was known as the "Hackney Rock".

"I went to Gayhurst road school with John Gardner, he was tough then. I met him about 25 years later in Hackney. He was a modest and very nice guy." – Anonymous

John Lewis Gardner was born on March 19th, 1953 in Hackney, England. He had an abusive father and his religious Italian mother protected him. His older brother was Alan Gardner, a gangster who worked for the London firms as a get-a-way driver in jewelry heists.

"He was the best getaway driver in the business and all the top firms wanted him. Not only was he a very fast driver, he was also extremely meticulous in planning the route before the raid. He left nothing to chance and became indispensable to the armed gangs because he could get them away from the scene in the blink of an eye. He had a reputation for not getting caught red handed. And they'd say: "Well, there's only one person who could have done that – Alan Gardner." – *The Forgotten Champ: John L. Gardner*

John L. Gardner began boxing at the Polytechnic Club, having his first amateur fight at age 18, winning his first fight by 2 – Round TKO, and he put together an unstoppable 14 – 0 record. It was in 1973 he won the North West London Amateur Heavyweight Title. He lost a very controversial decision to Dave McCann in the semi – finals for the London Championships in which a riot broke out at the Royal Albert Hall.

"I beat them all. I became a name. None of them wanted to fight me because of my reputation." – *The Forgotten Champ: John L. Gardner*

Afterwards, at age 20, he began his career as a professional boxer.

"Before I turned pro, no – one wanted to know me. I was an outcast, a pariah, one to be avoided.

Then I get a professional license and suddenly everyone wants to be my friend, birds start giving me the eye.

Fighters saw me as a man to be feared and avoided if possible. I was a name, but I still lived with me mum and I still had milk and chocolate at bedtime. And yes, I was still jealous of me brother's success with the girls." – *The Forgotten Champ: John L. Gardner*

On October 2nd, 1973, John L. Gardner defeated local journeyman Brian Hall, 9 – 15 – 2, by 2 – Round TKO at Royal Albert Hall in London, England. He put together a record of 6 – 0 (5 KO's) his first year in the ring. Gardner defeated the undefeated Les McGowan, 3 – 0, by 5 – Round TKO on March 26th, 1974 at Royal Albert Hall in London, England.

John L. Gardner, 10 – 0 (9 KO's), defeated undefeated Tony Mikulski, 8 – 0 by decision on points after 6 rounds at Royal Albert Hall in London, England. He then defeated Tony Blackburn, 13 – 4 – 1 by 8 – Round Decision. Afterwards, he defeated Peter Freeman, 10 – 3 by 6 – Round TKO.

He then knocked out contender Tony Mikulski in 3 rounds in a rematch and defeated American fighter Jerry Huston, Jr., 15 – 5, in October of 1975 by 5 – Round TKO due to a cut. On January 20th, 1976, Gardner knocked out veteran British journeyman Lloyd Walford, 27 – 35 – 4, by 2 – Round KO in London, England.

On March 2nd, 1976, Gardner defeated 6' 6 Norwegian fighter Bjorn Rudi, 15 – 1, by 3 – Round TKO.

John L. Gardner, 21 – 0 (16 KO's), faced hard hitting black British fighter Neville Meade, 12 – 5 – 1 (10 KO's) on October 26th, 1976 in London, England. Gardner defeated Meade by 6 – Round TKO, Meade being out on his feet. Afterwards, Meade would later become the British Heavyweight Champion.

Afterwards, on May 31st, 1977, Gardner defeated the African Heavyweight Champion, Ngozika Ekwelum, 12 – 3 – 5 (9 KO's) by 6 – Round TKO at Royal Albert Hall in Kensington, England.

"There was no great secret on my part – just ruthless, non – stop battery that beat the will out of 'em and sent their corner crazy. I felt like I couldn't lose." – *The Forgotten Champ: John L. Gardner*

John L. Gardner, 24 – 0 (20 KO's), was an undefeated professional heavyweight boxer and contender for the British and Commonwealth Heavyweight Titles. On September 27th, 1977, he was counted out in the first round by an American journeyman at Empire Pool in London, England. The referee let his opponent hit him with a sucker punch while the Englishman was talking to his corner.

Despite his first loss, he fought Denton Ruddock, 8 – 1, and defeated him by 8 – Round TKO for the Southern Area British Heavyweight Title on December 6th, 1977 at Royal Albert Hall in London, England.

"Gardner's relentless. He'll throw a punch every second of the round." – Sports writer Frankie Taylor

On October 24th, 1978, John L. Gardner, 26 – 1 (22 KO's), defeated Billy Aird, 19 – 11 – 5, by 5 – Round TKO due to retirement for the British and Commonwealth Heavyweight Titles, vacated by Joe Bugner. Aird was a tough fighter who floored the "Hackney Rock" in the first round. However, the tough John L. Gardner finished the show with his relentless pressure, forcing Aird to quit.

The legendary Jack Gardner, former Heavyweight Champion of Great Britain, the British Empire, and Europe from 1950 to 1952, died 18 days after his estranged relative John L. Gardner won the British and Commonwealth Heavyweight Titles.

John L. Gardner defeated American fighter Greg Sorrentino, 12 – 3 – 1 by 7 – Round TKO in December of 1978 and in February of 1979, he defeated 6' 4 American fighter Mike Koranicki, 21 – 3 – 2 by 9 – Round TKO, both in London, England.

"I was exterminating them one by one." – John L. Gardner

Afterwards, World Heavyweight Champion Muhammad Ali boxed three rounds in an exhibition match with him, and he described Gardner as a "very tough man".

On June 26th, 1979, John L. Gardner, 29 – 1 (25 KO's), defended his British and Commonwealth Heavyweight Titles against "Britain's Hardest Man", feared ex – convict Paul Sykes, 6 – 1 – 1 (4 KO's) at Empire Pool, in London, England. It was an action packed fight and perhaps the champion's best performance. Gardner battered Sykes round by round, making the bully turn away with a barrage of punches, the fight ending by 6 – Round TKO in front of a large crowd betting against him.

It was the fight John L. Gardner was most famous for during his career.

"It's a shame that people only remember the name John L. Gardner for a fight I had with some ex – con. I was champion of half the world, yet I became the man who fought Paul Sykes. He was small fry, but it seemed like he was the fucking star and not me. It's because he loved the limelight whereas I shunned it, and I believe that is why I became the forgotten champ." – *The Forgotten Champ: John L. Gardner*

On December 4th, 1979, the British fighter took a few steps up in competition against American heavyweight contender Jimmy Young, 23 – 9 – 2, and Gardner lost by 10 – Round Decision.

On April 22nd, 1980, John L. Gardner, 30 – 2 (26 KO's), fought Belgian fighter Rudi Gauwe for the (EBU) European Heavyweight Title and defeated him by 9 – Round TKO due to retirement.

He was the European Heavyweight Champion and a contender for the Heavyweight Championship of the World, while many in the United Kingdom believed John L. Gardner was the real Heavyweight Champion of the World.

On November 28th, 1980, John L. Gardner, 31 – 2 (27 KO's), defended his title against former Italian Heavyweight Champion, former European Heavyweight Champion and No. 5 Contender Lorenzo Zanon, 27 – 5 (9 KO's).

"The Italians hero – worshipped Zanon. They took the facking roof off when he walked into the Alpine arena, waving their little flags and singing his praises. They make a hell of a lot of noise, ya know, and he was king out there." – *The Forgotten Champ: John L. Gardner*

Zanon, a world title challenger had fought Larry Holmes, the WBC World Heavyweight Champion for the title and lost by 6 – Round KO, but while he was counted out, he was still conscious, getting up for the count, he returned to Italy to reclaim his vacated European heavyweight belt from John L. Gardner.

Gardner knocked out Zanon cold with a right hand, left hook in the fifth round, winning by spectacular 5 – Round KO, silencing his critics about his power, and defending his (EBU) European Heavyweight Title in Campione d' Italia, Lamobardia, Italy.

"BAM! I threw a jab over my left shoulder and came over with a right cross – smack on his chin. Then a left hook right on the top of his head. He was down, out cold." – John L. Gardner

"And Zanon was out like a light. He got counted out on his back. The Italians were mortified." – *The Forgotten Champ: John L. Gardner*

It was in March of 1981, John Gardner was set to face former World Heavyweight Champion, Muhammad Ali.

However, Muhammad Ali backed out after his license was revoked by the commission. Ali was all talk and he was defeated by Larry Holmes, his career being over. Most believe Gardner would have defeated Ali, and it certainly would have been a big notch on his record.

On March 17th, 1981, John L. Gardner, 32 – 2 (27 KO's), vacated his British and European Heavyweight Titles, and was now the No. 6 Contender for the World Heavyweight Title, fighting against Ossie Ocasio, 15 – 2 – 1 (10 KO's). The Puerto Rican had fought Larry Holmes for the WBC World Heavyweight Title. Ossie "Jaws" Ocasio bit the dust, being worn down and finished.

Gardner defeated Ocasio by 6 – Round KO, and a few years later, Ossie Ocasio became the reigning WBA Cruiserweight Champion of the World, being seen in retrospect as a title John L. Gardner probably could have won.

John L. Gardner, 33 – 2 (28 KO's), had defeated title challenger Lorenzo Zanon by 5 – Round KO (Larry Holmes finished him in 6 rounds); and Gardner defeated title challenger Ossie Ocasio by – 6 Round KO (Larry Holmes finished him in 7 rounds.)

On June 12th, 1981, Gardner fought undefeated American heavyweight contender, Michael Dokes, 20 – 0 – 1 (9 KO's) at Joe Louis Area in Detroit, Michigan.

Dokes, a large black man, standing 6' 3, weighing over 200 pounds, looked like he was in another weight class, compared to the short, stocky British fighter. Gardner was scrappy and landed a good right hand on Dokes' chin in the first, but in the fourth round, Dokes let out a combination, and with 23 unanswered punches, Gardner showed he had a good chin taking severe punishment.

The American caught the Englishman on the chin with a left hook that knocked his mouthpiece across the ring, and the "Hackney Rock" hit the canvas, the referee counting him out as he attempted to get back to his feet. John L. Gardner lost by 4 – Round KO and his hopes of getting his title shot on the world stage were set back.

He retired with a record of 33 – 3 (28 KO's) at 28 years old and moved with his wife to Tenerife, Spain where he began renting apartments. He opened a bar called "Ringside". However, two years later, Gardner made his comeback, defeating Ricky James by 2 – Round TKO and American fighter Lou Benson, Jr. by 8 – Round Disqualification.

On November 2nd, 1983, John L. Gardner fought 6' 4, Noel Quarless, 8 – 4, and lost by 2 – Round TKO at the Crest Hotel in London, England. Quarless landed a big right hand in the first round, and Gardner kept coming, looking game as ever. However, in the second round Quarless let out a barrage of punches against Gardner on the ring and the fight was stopped.

John L. Gardner retired at age 30 with a record of 35 – 4 (29 KO's), the former British, Commonwealth, and European Heavyweight Champion. He finished all of his title fights. Gardner defended his titles, undefeated as a champion.

After divorcing his wife, he removed back to England. American celebrities began touring with Planet Hollywood and he met legendary actor Sylvester Stallone a second time. The first meeting while Stallone promoted *Rocky II.*

"Sly had borrowed one of my classic moves for the third film, when he's fighting 'Clubber' Lang, played by the guy who was BA Baracus in the 'A Team'. It was the move where I jumped in with the left hook, feet off the ground, when the guy's shoulders come away from his chin. Stallone got it spot on." – John L. Gardner

On March 19th, 1993, his 40th birthday, he married Michelle Maddison and they had a daughter named Charlee and a son named Ross Luke Gardner who served as a Royal Marine and was also a professional light – heavyweight boxer.

John Gardner left Spain and began working as a salesman in Hinckley, England and removed to Newcastle where he was the top North East salesman for Pitney Bowes office and mailing equipment. He traveled from Venice to Colorado during that time. Gardner then worked for Alcatel in the late 1990s selling mobile phones.

Afterwards, he operated Newcastle Breweries Pub and on Halloween he was stabbed 14 times, his wife Michelle jumping on the assailant's back, being cut four times. The former prize – fighter had a punctured lung, a pierced spleen, his heart was narrowly missed and he was stabbed three times in the neck. However, due to his toughness, he survived.

The assailant was later sent to prison, released, and sent to prison again where he was stabbed to death.

Afterwards, John had kept a low profile, suffered from a heart attack in 2004 and was diagnosed with prostate cancer in 2013, as well as a blood clot in the lung, along with mild cognitive brain disorder, an early on – set dementia.

On March 19th, 2018, his 65th birthday, his memoirs titled, *The Forgotten Champ: John L. Gardner* was released.

I spoke with John L. Gardner and it was a pleasant conversation with the great champion fighter.

Courtesy to Derek Rowe for the photograph, and special thanks to John L. Gardner, his son Ross Gardner and his wife Mica Pullen Gardner for information.

References:
www.boxrec.com
The Forgotten Champ: John L Gardner by Nick Towle

TONY GARDNER

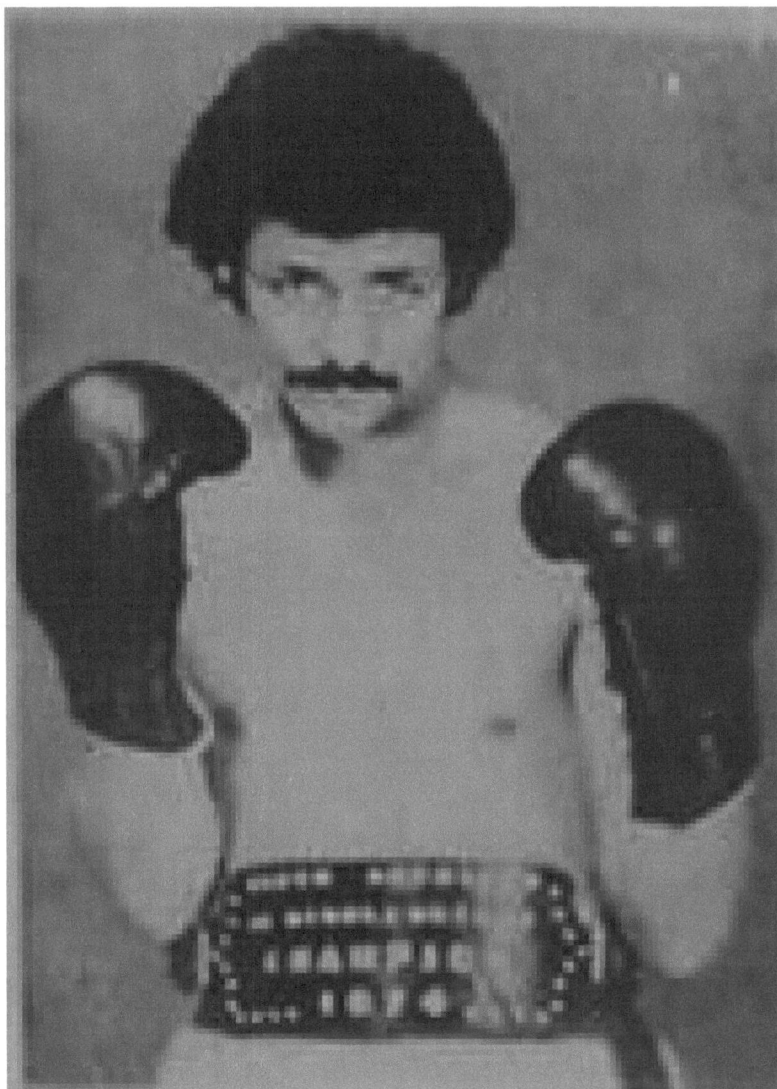

Tony Gardner, the "KO King", the North American Jr. Middleweight Champion, the Mid American Super Welterweight Champion, and the USA Tennessee State Super Welterweight Champion, was a top contender for the WBC Light Middleweight Title and the NABF Middleweight Title. He went from being a small-town hero to a title challenger. Gardner was a knockout artist who had a string of knockout victories from 1974 to 1976 that earned him the nickname, the "KO King".

A proud native of Memphis, Tennessee, standing six feet tall and weighing anywhere from 150 to 165 pounds, Gardner had knocked men out cold with his **"hellacious right hand"**. Although he had a baby face, Gardner had one shot knockout power. He was described as cagey with street smarts, hated to train, was fun to party with, and was known as a ladies' man.

GARDNER - VOL. III

Tony Lewis Gardner was born on December 2nd, 1946 in Memphis, Tennessee. His father was John Gardner, a rough man who had been a prize – fighter, policeman, and automobile dealer. His brother was Edward Gardner, standing 6' 1, weighing 225 pounds, and he was also a boxer.

He stated: **"Edward Gardner had one shot knockout power with his left hook, finishing his opponents in thirty seconds or less, and he could have went further than me, but he didn't like crowds, and he went to work for Roadway Truck Lines."**

John Gardner, a big puncher, taught his sons the manly art. It was during his youth he competed in four different weight classes, from bantamweight to junior middleweight. Tony Gardner won 6 Golden Gloves Championships in those divisions.

According to a newspaper, his amateur record was 43 – 4 – 1, possibly with even more fights. He served in the U. S. Army, being stationed in Germany. Afterwards, he began his career as a professional boxer.

On December 4th, 1969, Tony Gardner made his professional debut at 158 pounds against Lee Yankee Brown, 2 – 7 (2 KO's), in Fort Homer Hesterly Armory in Tampa, Florida. After four rounds, Gardner won by split decision. Sadly, in his next fight, he was knocked out in the first round in 1970 against Jimmy Jones, 0 – 1, in St. Louis, Missouri.

However, he bounced back with a victory over Bill Spicer in Oklahoma City. Sadly, he was knocked out in the first round against Adam Moore, 2 -1, in New Orleans, Louisiana. And again, he bounced back with a points victory over Toby Harrison the next year in 1971 in Tulsa, Oklahoma.

Gardner matched his record at 3 – 3 after he lost a points decision to Otis Dyer that year in Oklahoma City. His boxing career did not look promising at this point and it looked as if he were going nowhere. However, on October 2nd, 1971, Gardner earned his first knockout victory over Harold Brown, 4 – 8 – 2, after four rounds in Cushing, Texas.

It was from 1971 to 1973 that Gardner had twelve straight victories. On November 11th, 1971, he became the first man to knockout Simmie Black. And in his next fight, he knocked out Charlie Fischer in the second round in West Memphis, Arkansas.

Gardner knocked out Willie Johnson in the first round on February 12th, 1972 in West Memphis, Arkansas, his first opening round knockout victory. Then, he defeated Bobby Bell by KO in the first round in Oklahoma City. On September 5th, 1972, Gardner reversed a points decision against Otis Dyer after four rounds.

74

His 12 – fight winning streak ended on June 21st, 1972 after he was knocked out in the second round against the undefeated No. 1 Middleweight contender Tony Licata, 32 – 0 – 3, in Tampa, Florida. Gardner knocked out Harold Brown again in a rematch after three rounds in Mobile, Alabama, and then had two more losses, which included him being stopped in the second round against Canadian Middleweight Champion Dave Downey, 20 – 2 – 2, on September 4th, 1973 in Oklahoma City. It was after this loss, that he decided it was time to retire.

However, an Irish – American promoter named Pat O' Grady took an interest in the lanky bomber. On March 1st, 1974, Tony Gardner arrived in Oklahoma City and began what he called, **"My first true learning experience in boxing."** The Irishman O' Grady had Gardner sign up with a Texas Corporation called Starmaker, Inc., which hired heavyweight Claude "Humphrey" McBride to train the transplanted Tennessean who was now fighting out of Oklahoma City.

It was during the next three years Gardner would remain undefeated and prove himself as a viable fighter and title contender.

On April 9th, 1974, Tony Gardner began his reign as the "KO King" after knocking out light – heavyweight Cecil Peck in Dallas, Texas. Afterwards, Gardner had 19 straight knockout victories. As an undefeated fighter for three years, Tony Gardner had 25 victories, 22 by way of knockout.

His list of victims included three straight first round KO victories over Adam Moore, Jimmy Jones, and Billy Smith.

On May 9th, 1974, Tony Gardner knocked out Adam Moore cold in the first round in Enid, Oklahoma, avenging his loss. On May 21st, 1974, Gardner knocked out Jimmy Jones cold in the first round in Oklahoma City, avenging his loss. Gardner had his third straight first – round KO over Billy Smith in Dallas, Texas.

Gardner defeated former Texas Middleweight Champion Dave Burch, 16 – 8 (10 KO's) by 1 – Round KO.

One of the toughest opponents of his career was hard hitting Mexican knockout artist Sal Martinez, 28 – 5 – 1 (26 KO's). On August 20th, 1974 in Oklahoma City, Gardner knocked out Martinez in three rounds. It was Martinez's last fight.

On September 3rd, 1974, Tony Gardner defeated "Iron Man" Roy Christian 27 – 11 – 3 (12 KO's) by KO after a grueling 10 rounds.

The "KO King" defeated Roy Jones by 1 – Round KO in Oklahoma City before heading back to Memphis, Tennessee and knocking out tough light – heavyweight Ronnie Cichon. He then knocked out Jimmy Black and Bobby Brooks while in Oklahoma City. Afterwards, Gardner defeated Louisiana Welterweight Champion Emmett Atlas by 4 – Round KO at the Red Carpet Inn.

On December 5th, 1974, Tony Gardner, the "KO King", defeated "Iron Man" Roy Christian by KO in the final 15th round in Oklahoma City, Oklahoma for the North American Jr. Middleweight Title, a high ranking by the WBC, and he was now rated as No. 2 in the United States by Ring Magazine.

One of his corner men stated Gardner's fight with hard hitting Roy Christian was one of the best fights he had ever seen in all of his forty years of being involved in boxing, and the fight was described as **"perhaps the best ever seen in Oklahoma."**

Roy Christian stated: **"Tony Gardner is one of the hardest punchers I've ever faced. He hits harder than Dave Downey or Pat O' Connors combined."** Even his chief sparring partner, Rudy Jones, stated: **"Man, he don't hit like a middleweight, he thumps you like a heavyweight."** An Oklahoma City sportswriter stated: **"Few middleweights or light – heavyweights have the KO power that Gardner carries in his fists."**

The fans called Gardner one of the hardest punchers that they had ever seen.

Gardner stated: **"The fans, writers, and everyone has been real encouraging. Pat O' Grady is the man who made all of this possible. He believed in me when no one else did."**

The "KO King" began the year 1975 off well after he defeated Joe Adams by KO 42 seconds into the first round in Oklahoma City. The only man who was able to go the distance during Tony Gardner's reign of terror was Bobby Williams. Gardner defeated Williams twice, both by 12 – Round Decision.

On May 30th, 1975, he defeated Bobby Williams by 12 – Decision for the vacant USA Tennessee State Super Welterweight Title. He defeated him again on July 9th of that year in defense of the title. Then on January 20th, 1976, Gardner defeated Williams a third time by 15 – Round Unanimous Decision for the vacant Mid – American Super Welterweight Title, along with his North American Jr. Middleweight Title.

However, in 1976, his last victory was against Wayne Lewis after a 5 – Round TKO in Oklahoma City. The fight and the string of knockout victories made him a contender in the welterweight and middleweight divisions. His next fight was for the Middleweight Championship of the World.

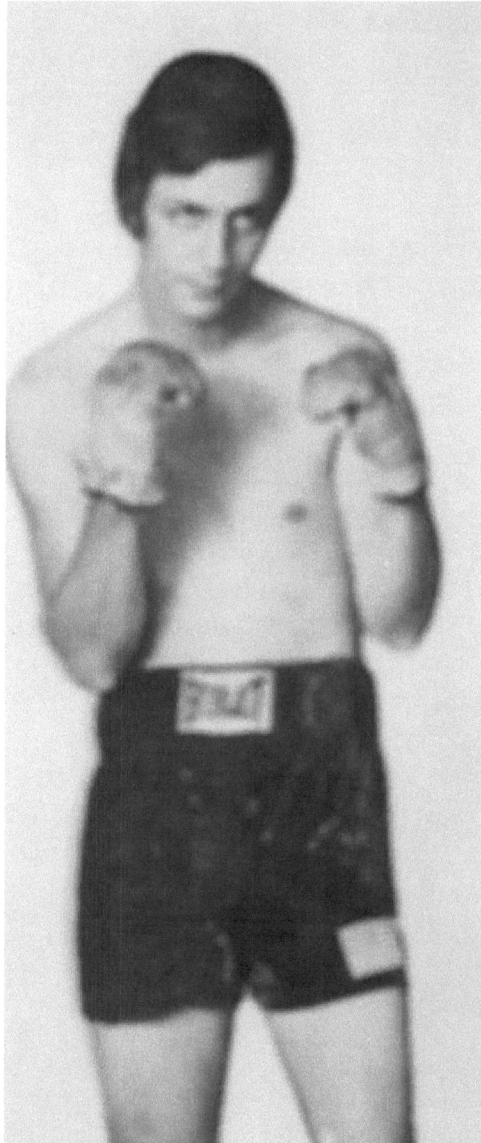

Tony Gardner, 41 – 6 (33 KO's) fought for the WBC Light Middleweight Title on February 28th, 1976 against Elisha Obed, 60 – 1 – 2 (43 KO's) in Nassau, Bahamas. Gardner beat Obed in the first round with hard roundhouse rights. Sadly, the "KO King" ran out of magic that day and his winning streak ended when he was hit with a right hand, being counted out in the second round.

However, he bounced back with two knockout victories in Oklahoma City. He traveled to Johannesburg, South Africa in June of 1976 in vain, because he was counted out in the first round. Then on May 3rd, 1977, he defeated Larry Brasier for the Mid – American Super Welterweight Title.

Gardner defeated Alfonso Aguirre with a first round KO in Oklahoma City and with seven straight victories, he had himself another title shot.

On May 25th, 1977, Tony Gardner, 51 – 11 (39 KO's), fought 6' 1, 155 – pound "Sugar Ray" Seales, 32 – 4 – 1 (18 KO's) for the NABF Middleweight Title in Anchorage, Alaska. He lost by 4 – Round TKO due to a cut. It was his last title shot and according to a fight poster before his fight with "Sugar Ray" Seales, Tony Gardner had a record of 55 – 9 (44 KO's).

The "KO King" had a string of losses afterwards due to suffering from rheumatism, becoming a journeyman, and his last fight was a 12 – Round Split Decision loss to Max Hord on July 12th, 1978 in Fernandina Beach, Florida. The "KO King", ended his career as a professional fighter with a record of 54 – 24 (42 KO's). However, this does not include club fights during his career.

It is said Gardner defeated 5 black belt Karate fighters all by first round knockout at the Rivermont in Memphis, Tennessee where he never lost a fight.

Gardner was a deadly striker, a tall, slim boxer with knockout power. He had several first round knockout victories; he had a hellacious, hard right hand. He was a contender, gatekeeper, and journeyman during his career as a professional fighter and afterwards was a cut man, promoter, and trainer, inducted into the Memphis Sports Hall of Fame.

I personally spoke to Tony Gardner over the phone. He was very personable with a great sense of humor, and speaks with a Southern drawl. I asked him if he knocked anyone out cold, and Gardner replied, **"If I caught 'em on the chin, I knocked 'em cold."**

Courtesy to Tony Gardner

References:
www.boxrec.com
University of Notre Dame

Chapter VIII: Athletes

"The athletic field and the gymnasium are the laboratories in which characters are molded. Competitive sports develop clear, quick – thinking judgement, a sense of fair play and respect for the rights of others, a conscientiousness that rules govern the game.

Athletics teaches us how to be good losers as well as good winners, and above all, teaches us good sportsmanship. All of these are very essential to your success in life after you have finished school and enter into the greatest game of all, that of earning a living. Many times you will find you are up against a stone wall and you can't gain a yard. Other times you will be thrown for a loss. It is then that your athletic experience will give you the courage to carry on, the spirit to fight on and overcome great odds and what seems like certain defeat, just as you did so many times in athletics." – Pink Gardner

LARRY GARDNER

Larry Gardner, the Baseball Star, was the greatest major league baseball player the State of Vermont ever produced. He was a four – time World Series champion. Gardner was the hero of the Boston Red Sox at the 1912 World Series Championships.

He had a .289 batting average; 1, 931 Hits, 934 Runs batted in; and 165 stolen bases. Gardner was handsome, humble, and had high morals; he stood 5' 8, weighed 165 pounds, and was one of the Boston Red Sox best third basemen.

"Gardner had a way of rising to the occasion as a trout rises to a fly in one of his favorite Vermont streams." – Tim Murnane

"There is no more modest, unassuming or clean young man in baseball than our Green Mountain boy, who is an honor and credit to the game and his state." – T. C. Cheney

"He has a disposition as sweet as the wild flowers that grow on the mountains of Vermont." – Tim Murnane

William Lawrence "Larry" Gardner was born on May 13th, 1886 in Enosburg Falls, Vermont. His father was Delbert Murancie Gardner, son of an Episcopal minister, from St. Armand Eastern Township of Quebec, Canada. Delbert Gardner was a "dealer in groceries, provisions, dry goods, Yankee notions, etc." He married Nettie Lawrence and they had three children, Dwight, Glenna, and Larry, being the youngest.

As a boy, he developed a lifelong passion for music, and especially fishing. Gardner attended Enosburg Falls High School and wrote for *The Echo*, a student magazine. It was as a high school student, he began his career in baseball. Gardner began his freshman year in 1902 and in his junior year he pitched every inning of every game and batted an even .400, Enosburg Falls being the **"champion high school in Franklin County."**

As a high school senior, Gardner told a reporter in 1943 during an interview that on May 22nd, 1905, pitching against Montpelier Seminary, stating: **"Of all the baseball I've ever been connected with, this particular game stands out most vividly in my mind."**

"Going into the ninth inning we were leading 1 to 0. "Montpelier Sam" was at bat with bases full and one out. I really was in a tough spot then. The man at bat knocked a hard one that I fielded. I forced the man out at home. The catcher threw to get the man out at first, making a double play and ending the ball game. I can tell you, the men at the corner drug store talked over this game for weeks."

Gardner finished second highest on the Enosburg Falls High School team that year with a .432 batting average. It was during the summertime he played in the Franklin County League. The *St. Albans Messenger* stated: **"'Larry' Gardner, the child marvel from Enosburg Falls, pitched rings around local baseball players yesterday at the local league grounds."**

It was in September of 1905, Larry Gardner, then 19 years old, attended the University of Vermont, where he majored in chemistry, his goal being to go out west to the gold mines and work as an assayer. According to *The Ariel* he was a **"peerless songster of the chem. lab., and because he is very mischievous Professor Nathan Merrill has required him to change his seat quite often in lectures."** The student paper later stated: **"His presence is a sure cure for the 'blues'."**

Gardner began his freshman year on the UVM baseball team along with another future major – leaguer named Ray Collins. On April 17th, 1906, Larry Gardner made an out in his first at – bat against Maine, becoming the first UVM batter in Centennial Field history, Vermont winning a 10 – 4 victory over Maine. The *Free Press* reported: **"Fielding features were contributed by Gardner and Collins, new men this year in the varsity line – up."**
After batting in each of his first 10 games as a collegian, Gardner led the UVM team with a .350 batting average. However, in his last seven games he batted .148 and committed 10 of 15 errors that season. His fielding percentage was .769 and batted .269, tying fourth on the squad, but he stole team – leading nine bases.

His reputation as a ball player was on the rise that summer, the *Free Press* stating: **"Gardner's brilliant plays for Vermont during his first year of college have attracted much attention."**

A major – league scout named George Winter dubbed Larry Gardner as a prospect, after seeing him play shortstop for UVM in 1907 with a .400 batting average in 11 games. However, on May 17th, 1907, at Centennial Field in the third inning of a game against Massachusetts Agricultural College, a player knocked a fly ball into left field, Higgins and Gardner both going after it. The men came together with terrific force. Gardner had his collar bone broken, while Higgins was knocked cold.

He missed the remainder of the season, the UVM student newspaper stating: **"Gardner will be sorely missed on the team. He was strong at the bat and wonderful at base running, his fielding was well-nigh errorless, while his throwing was swift and sure as fate."**

After his absence, UVM lost its next three games, finishing with a 10 – 7 record, but the next year Larry Gardner was elected Captain for his junior year and was elected President of the junior class for the coming school year. Gardner and Collins joined Bangor Cubs of the Maine State League during the summer. Fred Lake of the Boston Americans considered them big league material and Gardner established himself as Bangor's best hitter as the Cubs captured the 1907 pennant, the Vermont native finishing with a .371 average, leading the league.

The *Free Press* stated: **"Capt. Gardner, the hardest hitting man on the team, has been batting at a .300 clip, and it would be hard to find a better shortstop."**

(Courtesy to Albert Crisafulli and Love of the Game Auctions)

John Taylor, President of the Boston Americans, soon to become the Boston Red Sox, sent Gardner several offers by telegram, but Larry wanted to finish his senior year.

After final examinations, he gave up his senior year and reported to St. Louis where he became a Major League Baseball player at age 22 in on June 25th, 1908, replacing Harry Lord to play against the Washington Senators at Boston's Huntington Avenue Grounds.

Gardner hit a game – winning double in his first appearance as a Major League Baseball player.

Sadly, a few days later he played poorly against the New York Highlanders. The legendary Cy Young, 41 years old, gave the 22 – year old Vermont rookie advice sharing a bottle of rye whiskey called Cascades at a hotel bar. Then in July, he decided to gain more experience by playing for New England League's Lynn Shoemakers and in 61 games he batted .305 and in September he rejoined the Boston Red Sox, even returning to UVM for a semester for his senior year.

"With a little extra money in my pocket my senior year I lived the life of Reilly," he remembered. **"On occasion I'd even eat at Dorn's Restaurant, a high – class restaurant in town at that time. Heretofore I had eaten at any hash house."**

Although he was a major league ball player, he finished his senior year at UVM, going back to Burlington, Vermont for graduation, one of six to receive his Bachelor of Science in chemistry.

Gardner batted .297 with a .432 slugging percentage when he made it back to the field in 1909 in 18 more games. One sportswriter even stated, **"Gardner is one of the best second basemen in the country."**

Manager Patsy Donovan searched for a third baseman to replace Harry Lord, and manager Jimmy McAleer selected Larry Gardner third baseman on a team of American League all – stars. A Boston sportswriter stating: **"Third base has not been played so well in Boston since the days when Jimmie Collins was in his prime."**

Larry Gardner was in his prime during the 1912 season, hitting .315 with a team – leading 18 triples.

The Boston Red Sox played in the 1912 World Series. The Vermont native played poorly in the first three games against the New York Giants. However, in Game Four, he blasted a single and triple, scoring two runs in a 3 – 1 Boston victory. Afterwards, in Game Seven, Gardner hit Boston's only home run of the Series.

The final game of the Series, Game Eight at Fenway Park was tied 1 – 1 after nine innings. The New York Giants gained a 2 – 1 lead. The bases were loaded. Christy Mathewson, the pitcher, threw two low balls, and Gardner missed the third ball. The pitcher threw again and Gardner hit the ball in deep right field, the Boston Red Sox defeating the New York Giants for the 1912 World Series. Gardner stated: **"I was disappointed at first because I thought the ball was going out, but then when I saw Yerkes tag up, then score to end it, I realized I it meant $4, 024.68, just about double my earnings for the year."**

Game Eight at Fenway Park was one of the most dramatic games in baseball history, for which Larry Gardner will forever be remembered.

(Courtesy to Albert Crisafulli and Love of the Game Auctions)

He received a hero's welcome at Boston's Faneuil Hall, riding in a car with his father, greeted by 500 people. Olin Merrill, Chairman of the Vermont Republican Committee stated: **"Gardner is a clean type of ballplayer of whom any community might well feel proud."** The Burlington's Hotel Vermont honored Ray Collins, Olympian Albert Gutterson, and Larry Gardner. Among 450 in attendance, Governor Fletcher, Mayor Burke and about 300 UVM students, each of the guests of honor received a silver loving cup present by UVM President Guy Potter Benton.

From The City of Burlington
And The University of Vermont,
To "Larry" Gardner
In Loving appreciation of the deserved
Fame he has won for himself, for his
City and his alma mater as third baseman
For the Boston Americans,
World's Champions of 1912.

Afterwards, Gardner was named first – team third baseman on *Baseball Magazine's* All – America team, the first of four selections earned during the course of his career.

A reporter stated: **"Off the ball field Gardner prefers to read an essay on Shakespeare's poems than to discuss baseball."**

On July 11th, 1914, Larry Gardner collected three hits to a make a winner of rookie southpaw George Herman Ruth, the legendary Babe Ruth in his first big league pitching appearance. The two were even roommates. While Ruth was a pitcher, Gardner was an infielder.

On August 16th, 1916, *The Boston Globe* reported:

Babe Ruth beats Walter Johnson in great pitching duel
By T. H. Murnane

"By all odds the most interesting baseball game played at Fenway Park this year was provided yesterday afternoon, the champion Red Sox nosing out the Senators, 1 to 0, in 13 innings.

Walter Johnson was on the mound for the visitors and was never in better form or showed more stuff.

He was frequently cheered by the crowd, who figured that he was showing invincible form and, seemingly, overlooked the fact that "Babe" Ruth was going strong, clearing outpointing Johnson at the finish.

The winning run was driven in by Larry Gardner in the 13th, an inning that gave the crowd plenty of thrills and a finish that sent the fans home delighted."

Larry Gardner stated in an interview: **"How can you figure hitting? I still can't. One pitcher I never could touch was Eddie Plank. I got one hit off him in my entire career – and it won a ballgame. Yet I always could hit Walter Johnson and he was off in a class by himself. I did it by just punching the ball to the left field."**

He hit a .308 in the 1916 season and his batting average was fifth best in the American League, behind Tris Speaker, Ty Cobb, Shoeless Joe Jackson, and Amos Strunk. However, Gardner became the biggest hitter at bat in Boston's lineup as the Red Sox won their second consecutive AL pennant. And his reputation enhanced after he smashed two home runs in the 1916 World Series against the Brooklyn Dodgers.

Game Three, he hit a home run, Gardner stating: **"I hadn't been hitting hitting and I was really mad. Jack Coombs was pitching for the Dodgers and he was a helluva pitcher. He broke off a curve on me, a lefty hitter. I started to swing and tried to stop because I thought it was a bad pitch, but I was committed too far and had to go through with it. I even had my eyes shut. When I opened them, I saw the ball going over the wall. Can you believe that – hitting a home run with your eyes closed?"**

Game Four, Gardner hit a fastball from Rube Marquard giving the Boston Red Sox a 3 – 2 lead.

"That one blow, delivered deep into the barren lands of center field, broke Marquard's heart, shattered Brooklyn's wavering defense, and practically closed out the series." – Grantland Rice

The Boston Red Sox went on to win five games and again, Larry Gardner was the hero of the 1916 World Series.

Larry Gardner married Margaret Fourney, of Canton, Ohio, and despite being the hero of the Boston Red Sox, owner Harry Frazee could not give him a raise. He let his new bride visit him at spring training in Hot Springs, Arkansas as the club's guest. Gardner stated: **"I told my wife to take 40 baths a day and ride horses the rest of the time." "We really stuck Harry on that one!"**

Sadly in 1917, his batting average fell from .308 to .265 and it seemed his was slipping after 10 years on the Boston Red Sox. On March 1st, 1918, he was traded to the Philadelphia Athletics. Paul Shannon of the *Boston Post* wrote: **"The going of Gardner, one of the most powerful hitters on the team for years, one of its most dependable members and a model player in every way, will be severely felt."**

"The report that Gardner has passed the zenith of his career and is on the decline is all camouflage, probably designed to placate the Boston fans, with whom he was extremely popular. His moral and corrective influence upon the younger men of whom the team will mostly consist this year should be invaluable." – *Boston Globe*

He batted .285 at age 32 in the 1918 season and the Boston Red Sox barely won another World Series. One Boston reporter stated: **"Gardner's absence**

last year almost cost the Red Sox the world's championship, the Sox tired out more than a dozen third sackers in an attempt to fill his shoes."

However, he was traded by the Philadelphia Athletics in 1919 to the Cleveland Indians.

Gardner hit an even .300 and led the Cleveland Indians with 89 RBIs in the 1919 season, and in the 1920 season he batted .310 with a team leading 118 RBIs helping Cleveland finish on top of the American League.

A Cleveland Indians rookie named Joe Sewell stated: **"Larry Gardner helped me out a lot. He talked to me all the time when we were in the field, trying to steady me."** Sewell later became a Hall of Famer.

Larry Gardner won his fourth World Series Championship in 1920 for the Cleveland Indians.

On a road trip to Washington, D. C. during the 1921 season, the Cleveland Indians attended a White House reception to receive congratulations from President Warren G. Harding, from Ohio. When Gardner shook hands with the President, Harding said, **"I know you are a good player, young man, because way back in the early '80s I knew a player by that name. He was with Cleveland in the old National League and was a mighty good man."** Gardner, born in 1886, laughed and said, **"That was just about the time I was breaking in."**

Larry Gardner, at age 35, had his best season ever in 1921 establishing career highs for a .319 batting average, 101 runs, 187 hits, 32 doubles, and 120 RBIs. However, despite his prime and due to injuries, the 1922 season he batted .285 and began coaching. It was during his last two seasons from 1923 to 1924, he appeared in only 90 games. Gardner made his last Major League Baseball appearance on September 6th, 1924 at age 38 for the Cleveland Indians.
He invested in the Cape Cod cranberry business, which failed. Afterwards, he tried the automobile business in Enosburg Falls, and even owned a garage and Willys – Knight Dealership.

Gardner managed Dallas of the Texas League in 1925, but quit before the end of the season. He then managed Asheville of the South Atlantic League for two years. His son, Larry Gardner, Jr., stated that his father's chief complaint about the South: **"Those were the days before refrigeration, and he always said it was hard to find ice cream."**

After the 1927 season he returned to his garage and automobile business in Enosburg Falls, Vermont, and afterwards in 1929 he joined the physical education department at the University of Vermont.

Gardner became the head baseball coach at UVM and believed in sportsmanship ahead of winning, in two decades his team was 141 – 166, his son stating: **"I guess he liked the team to win, but all I remember was how warm and human he was with the players."**

He was named UVM's athletic director in 1942, he served as commissioner of the independent Northern League in the 1940s and as a part – time scout for the Boston Braves. Afterwards, he retired in 1952 and spent his retirement in Burlington, Vermont. He spent most of his retirement fishing for bass in Hogback Reef near the Colchester Lighthouse.

Gardner kept in touch with his fellow Major League baseball friends, his best friend being Harry Hooper.

Although he and Ty Cobb were rivals, they had steady correspondence in retirement. Gardner stated: **"I don't think Ty ever bunted for a hit against me because I found out his secret early. Cobb used to fake a lot of bunts, but I noticed that when he was really going to bunt, he always licked his lips. When I saw that, I'd start in with the pitch. He never realized I'd caught on."**

Larry and Margaret Gardner played golf at the Burlington Country Club, listened to music, and he was an avid reader. His favorite books were about World War II and during the war he kept a map on which he pinpointed the advance of Allied forces, but discontinued after his son John Gardner was drafted.

William Lawrence "Larry" Gardner died at age 89 on March 11th, 1976 in his son's home in St. George, Vermont. He left his body to the UVM's Department of Anatomy and his body was cremated. His ashes were spread at St. Paul's Cathedral in Burlington, Vermont.

Larry Gardner was an original inductee into the University of Vermont's Hall of Fame in 1969 and *Collegiate Baseball* named him the third baseman on its all – time All – America team. Then in 1973, SABR conducted a survey of its members to determine the greatest baseball player born in each state, legendary baseball star Larry Gardner being selected from Vermont. The UVM's most valuable player award in baseball was named after him and the UVM's cage, along with Ray Collins.

Strangely, he was never inducted into the National Baseball Hall of Fame, despite being the hero for the Boston Red Sox in two World Series Championships, and a four-time World Series Champion.

Larry Gardner, Jr., stated: **"I remember when Harry Hooper was being considered for the honor and Dad talked with me after I raised the**

question about his being eligible for it. Generally speaking, Dad was very quiet, soft – spoken, reticent about his baseball career when talking with me, but at that time he got very talkative – very adamant – and told me, "If you boys ever get involved with the campaigning, the politics of getting me into the Hall of Fame, I'll be upset and angry."

The UVM baseball team in 1986 wore commemorative patches on their sleeves in honor of his 100th birthday and a regional chapter of SABR was founded in the Green Mountains in 1993, its members elected to call it the Larry Gardner Chapter, and in 2012, he was inducted into the Vermont Sports Hall of Fame.

Larry Gardner was inducted in 2000 into the Boston Red Sox Hall of Fame.

Courtesy to Albert Crisafulli and Love of the Game Auctions for photographs

References:
www.loveofthegameauctions.com
www.sabr.com
Green Mountain Boys of Summer: Vermonters in the Major Leagues 1882 – 1993
edited by Tom Simon
National Baseball Hall of Fame Library
University of Vermont

JIMMY GARDNER

Jimmy Gardner, the Hockey Player, was a founder of the National Hockey League. He also founded the Montreal Canadiens, suggesting the team's name. Jimmy Gardner was inducted into the Hockey Hall of Fame.

James Henry Gardner was born on May 21st, 1881 in Montreal, Quebec, Canada. He stood 5' 9, weighed 180 pounds, and began his career as a hockey player with the Montreal Hockey Club amateur men's team in 1900 with the Canadian Amateur Hockey League. Gardner played until 1903 winning the Stanley Cup twice.

Then in 1903, the players from Montreal Hockey Club left to form the new Montreal Wanderers of the Federal Amateur Hockey League (FAHL) and after one season, he turned professional.

Gardner became a professional hockey player in 1904, his position being Left Wing, and he played two years for the U. S. Teams known as the Calumet Miners and the Pittsburgh Professionals before returning to Canada.

He then played for the Montreal Shamrocks and in 1908 he returned to the Wanderers, winning the Stanley Cup in 1908 and 1910 twice. Afterwards, he left in 1911 and joined the new PCHA, playing for New Westminster for two seasons and then returned to Montreal to play for the Montreal Canadiens for two seasons. Gardner had played for the Calumet Miners, Pittsburgh Professionals, Montreal Shamrocks, Montreal Wanderers (winning two Cups), New Westminster Royals, and the Montreal Canadiens, from 1913 to 1915 serving as captain.

Afterwards, he coached the Montreal Canadiens for two seasons and in his later years he was Head Coach of the Hamilton Tigers, as well as teams in the Western Canada Hockey League and Quebec Hockey League.

Gardner founded the Montreal Canadiens in 1909, including its name, he and Ambrose O' Brien worked on the idea of the new National Hockey Association and a new French team named 'Les Canadiens'.

Jimmy Gardner was a professional hockey player from 1899 to 1915, retired and from 1910 to 1924, was a hockey coach.

On November 6th, 1940, Jimmy Gardner died at age 59 in Montreal, Quebec, Canada.

It was in 1963, he was inducted into the Hockey Hall of Fame.

Photograph is public domain.

References:
www.wikipedia.com
www.hockey-reference.com
www.legendsofhockey.com
Hockey Hall of Fame (2003). Honoured Members: Hockey Hall of Fame. Bolton, Ontario: Fenn Publishing

GOLDIE GARDNER

Goldie Gardner, the Racecar Driver, was an Englishman who was awarded the BRDC Gold Star three times during his career. He was a speed king of his era. Gardner was the first to exceed 200 mph in a light car.

Alfred Thomas Goldie Gardner was born on May 31st, 1890 in Woodford Green, Essex, England. He was known as Goldie, which was his mother's maiden name. Gardner was educated at Pelham House and Uppingham School.

Then in 1910 he embarked from England to Colombo, Ceylon for a three-year business appointment in Katha, Burma, but suffered from typhoid fever with malaria, being sent back to England on six months' leave.

Gardner enlisted in September of 1914 and was granted a commission in the Royal Artillery as a Second Lieutenant. He had a distinguished military career and was the youngest officer in the British Army to earn the rank of Major.

Gardner was wounded, receiving injuries to his right hip and leg in August of 1917 when his reconnaissance plane was shot down, later being discharged in 1921 as medically unfit for further service.

After the war, in 1924, Goldie Gardner purchased a Gordon England special Austin Seven and despite his disabled leg, he began his racing career on the British circuits. He teamed up with MG Cars and was a successful racer. However, in 1932, the disability of his leg was worsened after a crash at the RAC Tourist Trophy race in Northern Ireland.

Once he recovered in 1934, Gardner continued his career and placed third in the 500-mile race at Brooklands, winning the 1, 100c class. He accompanied Sir Malcolm Campbell's expedition to Daytona Beach, Florida in 1935 and witnessed the World Land speed record attempt, then returned to England where he focused on speed racing records. On March 10th, 1936, he married Mary Eleanor King Boalt in Daytona Beach, Florida. She was an heir of the J. R. Watkins company in Winona, Minnesota. However, in 1940, they divorced.

On his 49th birthday, May 31st, 1939, Goldie Gardner drove his special engineered MG in Dessau, Germany and won the 750cc up to 1, 100cc class records over 2 kilometers, 1 mile, and 5 kilometers distances, at average speed records of 203.5 mph, 203.3 mph, and 197.5 mph.

On June 2nd, 1939, Gardner gained the 1, 100cc to 1, 500cc class records over the same distances at average speeds of 204.3 mph, 203.9 mph, and 200.6 mph.

Then in 1940, he remarried to Una Eagle – Clarke and they had one daughter in 1958 named Rosalind Gardner.

Gardner offered his service during World War II and was commissioned as a Second Lieutenant in the Mechanical Transport Training, earning the rank of Major and then in 1942 he was promoted to Lieutenant Colonel.

It was between 1936 and 1950, he set over 100 international and local speed records throughout the United Kingdom, Europe, and the United States.

Then in September of 1948, before the announcement of Jaguar's new engine he broke the flying mile, kilometer, and five – kilometer Class E records on the new motor road near Ostend. It was an experimental Jaguar 2 – liter 4 – cylinder. Gardner's new records were mile 173.678 mph, kilometer 177.112 mph, and five kilometers 170.523 mph.

He wrote and published a book titled *MAGIC M. P. H.*

It was in 1951, Gardner had his supercharged MG streamliner EX – 135 car and in Bonneville Salt Flats, Utah, he earned 6 international and 10 American records in the 1, 100cc to 1, 500cc engine class and in 1952 he returned to Bonneville with his MG EX – 135 car and set 21 speed records in the same engine he had used the previous year.

Sadly in 1952, he suffered a cerebral hemorrhage and was forced to retire from motor sports. Gardner was awarded the British Racing Drivers' Club gold star in 1938, 1947, and in 1949, as well as the Segrave Trophy which is awarded to anyone who demonstrated "Outstanding Skill, Courage and Initiative on Land, Water and in the Air".

Goldie Gardner earned the Segrave Trophy in 1938, his citation reads: **"For attaining the class G land speed record of 186.6 miles per hour (300.3 km/h) in a 1100cc MG Magnette on the German autobahn."**

Photograph is public domain retrieved October 31st, 2022 at
https://en.wikipedia.org/wiki/File:Colonel_Goldie_Gardner.jpg

References:
MAGIC M. P. H. by Lt. Col. A. T. Goldie Gardner, O. B. E., M. C.
Royal Automobile Club archives
British Racing Drivers Club

RACECAR DRIVERS

Chester Leroy "Chet" Gardner was born on March 16th, 1898 in Grant City, Missouri.

He was an American racecar driver, named by promoters as "The Grand Old Man of Auto Racing".

Chet Gardner began racing in 1922 in Colorado and in 1933, he won the Midwest AAA Sprint Car Championship, being named "Southern Dirt Racing King" twice.

It was between 1928 to 1938, he made 25 starts in the AAA series, and in 1930 to 1938, he competed in the Indianapolis 500 before his death.

Chet Gardner died on September 3rd, 1938 in Flemington, New Jersey, in an accident during a time trial at the Flemington Fair Speedway when he swerved to avoid hitting a child that had ran onto the racetrack.

He was survived by his wife Fannie M. Gardner, along with his three brothers, Dead Orville Gardner, Ray Alva Gardner, and Paul Theodore Gardner.

William H. "Speed" Gardner was born on July 2nd, 1895 in East Liberty, Pennsylvania.

He was an American racecar driver during the AAA era and was a relief driver for Chet Gardner.

"Speed" Gardner died on April 25th, 1972 in Bayonet Point, Florida.

Frank Gardner was born on October 1st, 1931 in Sydney, New South Wales, Australia.

Gardner was best known for touring car racing, winning the British Saloon Car Championship three times, along with being a sports car racing driver. He was the European Formula 5000 champion, participating in nine World Championship Formula One Grands Prix. Frank Gardner was described as the toughest racecar driver in Australia.

He died at age 77 on August 29th, 2009 in Mermaid Waters, Queensland, Australia.

Wayne Michael Gardner was born on October 11th, 1959 in Wollongong, New South Wales, Australia.

He is an Australian professional Grand Prix motorcycle and touring car racer.

Gardner won the 1987 500 cc Motorcycle World Championship, being the first Australian to win motorcycling's premier class.

His success on the world motorcycle road racing circuit earned him the nickname *The Wollongong Whiz.*

His sons Remy Gardner and Luca Gardner are motorcycle racers.

Racecar drivers surnamed Gardner:
Chet Gardner, "The Grand Old Man of Auto Racing"
Goldie Gardner
Frank Gardner, Australian racecar driver
William "Speed" Gardner
Walson Gardner, NASCAR driver
Wayne Gardner, Australian motorcycle champion
Slick Racin Gardner, stunt driver

References:
www.wikipedia.com

HANDSOME JACK GARDNER

Handsome Jack Gardner, the Basketball Coach, was one of the greatest coaches in the history of the sport. He is ranked #27 greatest basketball coach. Gardner was known as "The Fox" and is the only coach in history to have led two different schools to the NCAA Final Four two times each.

Jack Gardner

"Controversial at times, Jack Gardner was the ideal coach to resurrect the fortunes of basketball at Kansas State University." – Steve Farney

James Hamlin Gardner was born on March 29th, 1910 in Texico, New Mexico. He was the son of Rev. George McDowell Gardner and Nancy Kemp who removed from Barnesville, Lamar County, Georgia to Tehama County, California. His grandfather was Maj. Robert Beall Gardner, a Confederate officer and surgeon during the Civil War, the son of Sterling Gardner of Warren County, Georgia.

His lineage dates to Thomas Gardner (1721 – 1773) of Halifax County, North Carolina.

Jack Gardner attended college from 1928 to 1932 where he played basketball, graduating from the University of Southern California and then he began his career as a coach.

It was from 1939 to 1942, he coached at Kansas State, winning three conference crowns and captured two Big Eight Holiday Tournament championships. He rejoined as coach in 1946 and his 1950/1951 team finished 25 – 4 and lost in the finals of the NCAA tournament to the University of Kentucky. Arguably, his team was the best in Kansas State history and he left in 1953 after compiling a 147 – 81 record with the Kansas Wildcats.

Afterwards, he left Manhattan, Kansas and was head coach at the University of Utah, remaining there for 18 years. He led the Utes to the NCAA Tournament six times and in 1961 as well as 1966 had two Final Four appearances. Gardner finished his career winning seven conference titles, from 1959 to 1962 compiling a 72 – 14 record. He finished at Utah with a 339 – 154 record.

"Handsome Jack" Gardner finished his career in 1971 with an overall career college coaching record of 486 – 235, winning 3 Big Six/Seven regular seasons in 1948, 1950, and 1951; 6 Skyline regular seasons in 1955, 1956, 1959, and 1962; and in 1966 a WAC regular season.

He was a member of the Naismith Basketball Hall of Fame, the Kansas Sports Hall of Fame in 2000, Southern Utah Hall of Fame, Utah All – Sports Hall of Fame, State of Utah Basketball Hall of Fame, Helms Foundation Hall of Fame, Kansas State University Hall of Fame, the Crimson Club (University of Utah), the Modesto Junior College Hall of Fame, the Redlands High School Hall of Fame, and in 2006 into the College Basketball Hall of Fame.

Coach Gardner was inducted in 1984 into the Basketball Hall of Fame and was a recipient of the National Basketball Coaches' Golden Anniversary Award.

On April 9th, 2000, he died at age 90 in Salt Lake City, Utah.

He was survived by his son James Bruce Gardner.

"*Sports Illustrated* once wrote that Jack Gardner "could win with an old man on the post and four midgets." Dubbed "The Fox" during his tenure at Utah, Gardner was an expert in fast break hoops and a promoter of fundamental basketball. He won nearly 70 percent of his games. While only a handful of coaches have taken more teams to the Final Four, Gardner was the first coach in history to lead two different schools to appearances in the Final Four twice each. He first led Kansas State to the Final Four in 1948 and 1951. Then, in 1961 and 1966, he again brought his Utah team, "the Runnin' Redskins" to Final Four placements. Gardner also popularized basketball in the Pacific Northwest with his success at Utah. In 28 seasons of college basketball, Gardner experienced only three losing seasons and compiled ten 20-win campaigns." – www.hoophall.com

References:
It's Time to Play: Jack Gardner, Basketball and KSU by Steve Farney
www.hoophall.com/hall-of-famers/jack-gardner
Naismith Memorial Basketball Hall of Fame

PINK GARDNER

Pink Gardner, the Wrestler, was the Middleweight Champion of the World and the Light Heavyweight Champion of the World during his career. He was a wrestler, lawman, and politician. Gardner was a "master of leverage", a true American champion, a man who set a goal and achieved it by sheer perseverance.

"In my wrestling career, I learned that success was based upon preparedness. I have never forgotten the lesson." – Pink Gardner

A tired opponent once grunted, **"That guy turned me against myself. My own muscles beat me!"**

The Schenectady County Union Star sportswriter Dan Duval stated:

"Carroll 'Pink' Gardner, Schenectady's claimant to the middleweight wrestling championship, is preparing for a strenuous campaign on the mats that will take him to all parts of the country.

"Pink" Gardner is one of the leading middleweight wrestlers of the world and his ability to more than hold his own with any of the famous grapplers in his class is known wherever the wrestling game flourishes. He has met and defeated all of the leading lights in the middleweight division, as well as hundreds of grapplers who are not so well known.

"Pink" is probably in his prime now. He is still a young man in years, but a veteran in experience. For several years past he has been campaigning actively on the mats in cities from coast to coast and from the Gulf to the northern border of the States. Breaking in a few years ago as a preliminary boy, he rose quickly to the front ranks, and his name is familiar to thousands of followers of the wrestling game in all sections of the country.

Even in defeat, Pink has won the praise of many sportswriters, fans and opponents because of his great work on the mat. Promoters make no mistake in booking Gardner, for he is conscientious and believes in giving service.

Gardner is the acme of physical perfection and never was in better shape for strenuous wrestling than he is at the present time. Dressed in street clothes, one would never imagine the powerful sinews and muscles he possesses. Physical experts consider him one of the most perfect specimens of physical man outside of the great Sandow. Gardner may even be superior to Sandow, for Gardner's body is more in proportion to his height of five feet, eight inches. Sandow was also of the same height, but his neck and biceps were much too large for a man of his height. Pink is more nearly correct, according to Sandow's system of measurements, as his neck measures 16 inches and biceps 14 ½ inches.

Gardner, as all those who have watched him wrestle know, is like chain lightning. He is unusually aggressive and works at a relentless pace that, with few exceptions, wears out his opponent. He is a quick thinker and his brain – work has netted him many victories over men who are less quick to size up the situation. He has the stamina that is necessary to carry him through the hours of grueling wrestling with heavier and stronger opponents. For a man of his build, he has shown almost superhuman strength in extricating himself from precarious positions when it seemed certain he was doomed to defeat.

Above all things, Pink Gardner is a true representative of the ideal American sportsman. He is always out to win, but only by fair means. Never has a well – substantiated report reached the writer of Pink being anything but sportsmanlike..."

Carroll Altz Gardner was born in 1894 in Poughkeepsie, New York. His father, Charles Nelson Gardner was a monument dealer who removed the family to Schenectady, New York. It was here that "Pink" Gardner became a hometown hero.

He earned his nickname either from wrestling with other boys and his skin turning beet red afterwards, or it was from being an admirer of a fighter known as "Pinky" Baker, or for perhaps being in good physical shape. His first job was selling newspapers, and then he drove a milk and bakery wagon. It was at one time he owned a small restaurant and was a member of all of the Masonic bodies, Odd Fellows, Elks, Mohawk Club, and was even President of the Exchange Club.

Gardner began wrestling at age 17 at the YMCA in 1911 while on a semi – professional football team. He combined regular mat workouts with strenuous labor at his father's monument business. After two years of wrestling at the YMCA, at age 19, "Pinky" Gardner made his debut as a professional wrestler, at 5' 8, 140 pounds in a welterweight preliminary to the Waldek Zybysko – Dr. Roller main event at the Hudson Theater.

His amateur bouts earned him a following. Gardner pinned his opponent and left the ring proud of his victory. He earned his first fight purse – a dollar and a half.

Gardner, standing 5' 8, weighing 162 pounds with a neck that measured 16 inches, chest 41 expanded to 44 ½, waist 31, biceps 14 ½, forearm 12 ½, thigh 22, and calf 14 ½ inches, began taking dollar – a – minute challenges at carnivals to make quick money. He climbed his way up the middleweight ladder at the same time with his father as his manager. And when carnival season ended, he worked as a landscaper.

A newspaper in Kent, Ohio noted: **"Pink" Gardner, whose business activities have previously been confined to the saw dusted mat at the City Auditorium, has cast in his lot with the corps of tree surgeons operating in this city. Mr. Gardner reports frankly with regard to his novitiate, that he feels much more at home in the friendly shelter of a toehold, than in the swaying branches of a Mecklenburg patient."**

On December 15th, 1916, at the Lyceum Theater in Washington, D. C., "Pinky" Gardner fought Joe Turner for the World's Middleweight Wrestling Championship. He had wrestled for five years, three years as a professional, and at age 22, he was a contender and title challenger. However, the respectable champion Joe Turner kept his belt, but "Pinky" Gardner made him work to keep the title and won admiration, the sportswriters recognizing him, praising his lighting speed, ability in the ring, and his gentlemanliness outside of the arena.

The Schenectady presses screamed: **"PINK GARDNER, Phenomenal Middleweight Wrestler"**. Gardner and Turner met two years later in a rematch which ended in a draw after two hours and 45 minutes, the longest bout of Pink's career. The shortest bout of his career was when Gardner broke an opponent's leg in just six and a half minutes into the fight at Battle Creek, Michigan.

His father's dream occurred in 1917 when he purchased property at 918 State Street which developed into the monument business known as Charles N. Gardner & Sons and as a shooting star, professional fighter "Pink" Gardner divided his time between bouts on the road and work at the monument business at home before he earned a title shot.

On April 11th, 1918, "Pinky" Gardner lost to Mike Yokel for the Middleweight Championship of the World in Boston, Massachusetts. However, he persevered. It is perseverance which made him a champion.

On February 27th, 1921, "Pink" Gardner defeated Finnish wrestler Waino Ketonen for the Middleweight Championship of the World in Boston, Massachusetts. However, on November 23rd, 1921, he lost to Ira Dern in Salt Lake City, Utah. And on December 1st, 1921, he lost his World Middleweight Title to Walter Miller in Los Angeles, California.

"Pink" Gardner reclaimed his World Middleweight Title after he defeated Mike Yokel in 1922 in Boston, Massachusetts. The Atlantic City Press stated: **"... But while Gardner has a perfect physical body, in his skull he carries a brain that is unusual. He has a quick – thinking mind, a clear eye and a forceful determination and gameness that would make him a captain of industry if he should take up and devote all his time to business..."**

After proving himself as the World's Middleweight Champion Wrestler, Gardner suffered a leg injury after slipping through ice and which kept him off the mat for 18 months.

His brother and mother died in the 1920's, and after the death of his father in 1926, he became President of Charles N. Gardner & Sons.

"Pink" Gardner at 5' 8, weighing 175 pounds, retired the World's Middleweight crown and was now a contender for the World's Light – Heavyweight Title.

On August 6th, 1923, *The Schenectady Gazette* reported:

PINK GARDNER TO HELP JACK FOR TRAINING
Local Wrestler Will "Rough Up" Dempsey in Final Fortnight Before Firpo Bout.

"Pink" Gardner, local middleweight wrestler, will assist Jack Dempsey, heavyweight champion, to prepare for his coming title bout with Luis Angel Firpo, Argentine contender for the honors, at the Polo Grounds in New York next month, it was learned yesterday following a visit of "Pink" and his brother, Pete, and Lewis McCue, a friend of the Gardner brothers to Dempsey's training camp at White Sulphur Springs, Saratoga Lake.

The Gardners and McCue went in bathing with the champion and spent an enjoyable time with Jack. Dempsey introduced to Gardner by McCue, marveled at Pink's physique and stated he would like to have him appear at his camp during the first two weeks' in September in order to assist him in his working out and Gardner readily consented. The champion figures a fighter needs such "roughing up" that a wrestler can give him to get in proper condition for a fight.

In preparing for his bout with Georges Carpentier two years ago Dempsey worked out with "Bull" Montana, but the "Bull" has been obliged to retain from mixing with boxers or wrestlers owing to his contract with a moving picture concern. Montana has a pair of beautiful "cauliflower" ears and according to physicians, could lose them through injury, and the motion picture producers would not use "Bull" minus ears. Hence, the reason for his non – appearance with Dempsey again and Gardner's appointment as successor.

On August 24th, 1927, Gardner defeated Clarence Eklund for the Light – Heavyweight Championship of the World at Columbus, Ohio, as recognized in the region.

He was tapped by Stadiums Unlimited to compete as one of the world's top wrestlers in an elimination tournament. On October 28th, 1928, Gardner defeated Mike Yokel in Sydney, Australia. He battled through six eliminations, but placed in 2nd to Clarence Eklund of Tulsa, Oklahoma in the World's Light – Heavyweight International Tournament in 1928 in Melbourne, Australia.

However, the *Melbourne Herald* praised him as **"The Gene Tunney of the Mat"**. He traveled through Ceylon, India, Egypt, Italy, France, and England, before returning to America. Afterwards, he returned to his monument business and was approached by the Mayor of Schenectady to try politics.

Carroll "Pink" Gardner, the hero of his hometown of Schenectady, was elected by 6, 000 votes in 1931 at age 37 as Sheriff of Schenectady County, New York, the first Democrat to win office in 21 years. It was during his term in office from 1931 to 1934, Sheriff Gardner began cleaning up corruption, cleaning up the jail, and he uniformed his officers. It was during a raid on a gambling establishment, one of his deputies smilingly observed that the sheriff was **"just as good with an ax on a slot machine as he was with a step – over toe hold in the ring."**

As the owner of Charles N. Gardner & Sons monument business he had a marble two – story stone built at 918 State Street which states:

"Charles Nelson Gardner, A Gifted Craftsman, Laid the Foundation for this Establishment in 1900. This Building is Dedicated by His Children in Loving Memory of a Devoted Father, as a Tribute to His Vision, Integrity and Perseverance and as a Monument to his Achievements, May 22, 1931."

"Pink" Gardner, the former Middleweight Champion of the World, fought boxer turned wrestler, "Gentleman" John Kilonis in April of 1932 at the Camden Garden for the World's Light – Heavyweight Wrestling Championship. As the 38 – year old sheriff made the champion Kilonis look foolish in front of a roaring crowd of 3, 000 fans, the quick tempered John Kilonis began to swing punches at "Pink" Gardner. The referee stopped the bout disqualifying Kilonis.

Gardner won the Light – Heavyweight Championship of the World in 1932 in Camden, New Jersey.

It was a good year for him, because he married young Eleanor Lunn, the daughter of the Schenectady politician Rev. George Lunn. The vows were exchanged at 8 p.m. on July 20th, 1932 at the First Presbyterian Church. His wife described her headlining husband Mr. Gardner as a wonderful man with big cauliflower ears, who wears a gun, and owns a monument business.

Beach Haven Times of New Jersey reported: **"Light – Heavy Wrestling Champ Married."**

1924

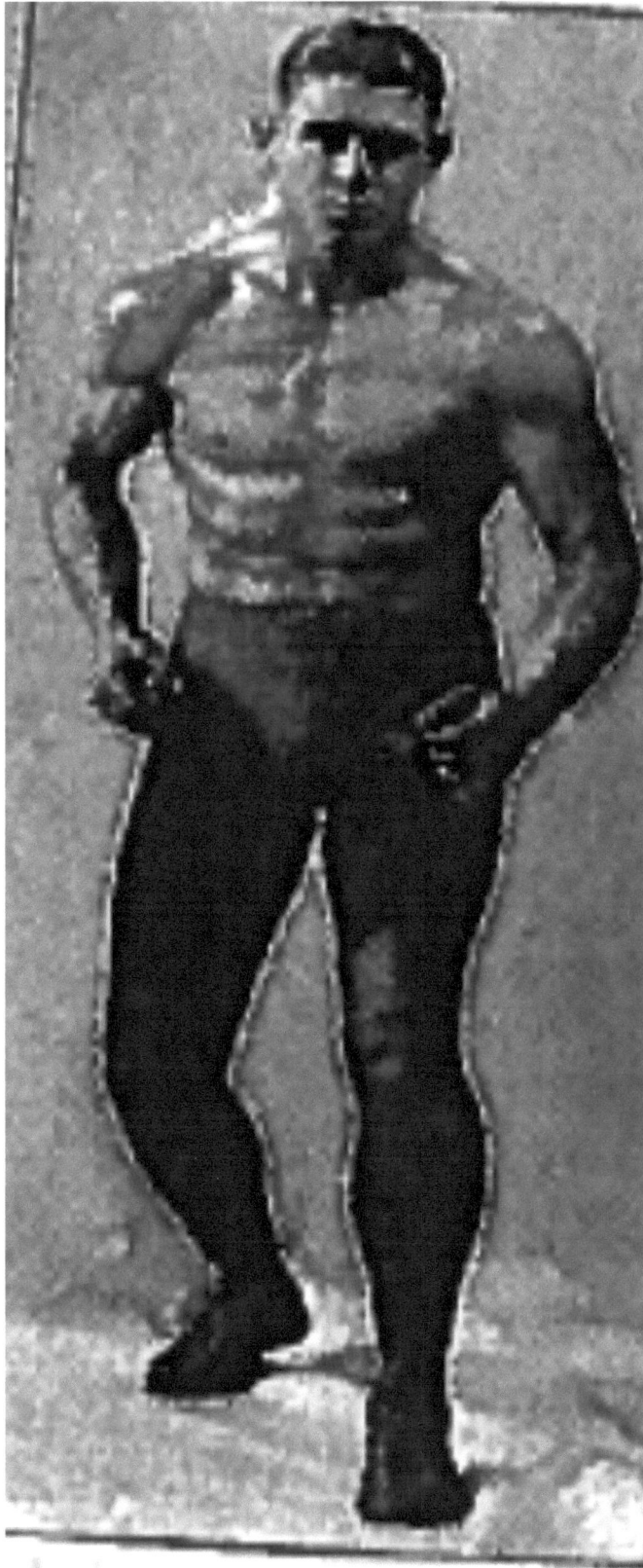

"Pink" Gardner at age 38 in 1932 when he was the World's Wrestling Light – Heavyweight Champion.

On October 13th, 1932, Gardner defended his World's Light – Heavyweight Title in 1932 after defeating the "Blond Tiger", Carl Van Wurden, the Canadian Light – Heavyweight Champion, in front of a crowd of 2, 000 fans in the largest indoor wrestling crowd in Halifax history at Halifax, Nova Scotia Arena. W. J. Foley of the *Halifax Chronicle* reported:

GARDNER OUTCLASSES WURDEN TO RETAIN TITLE

"Sheriff Pink Gardner, who is world's light – heavyweight mat champion in many states, erased Carl Van Wurden from the outstanding challenger lot last night at the Arena.

Gardner, winning in straight falls, proved himself in a class above the Ottawa boy. This here Gardner boy looks the part. He is a smooth – looking guy and a smooth worker. One cannot tell just how things are going with him and on two occasions, when it looked as though Wurden would pin the Yankee with his more or less famous airplane spin, Pink slipped out of the hold and pinned Wurden's shoulders to the mat.

Gardner is every inch the champion. He is too good for Wurden, good as the Ottawa boy is. I picked Wurden to win, because Carl is a good wrestler, but I had never seen Gardner in action. He's worth watching."

"...There wasn't so much in the second fall. Wurden, trying hard to even up the match, chased Gardner around the ring before getting a hold that enabled him to hold the sheriff aloft. Again the hold was not a perfect one. Gardner had one of his hands free. He slipped out of the hold, fell atop the Canadian and won the fall. The sheriff had gotten his man again. The time was four minutes, five seconds." "In fact at times Gardner made it look as though he was only foolin', which of course he was not doing. But he seemed to be foolin' and the fans got a kick as he stepped around the ring with the grace of a panther and the arrogance of a champion. Champions, they tell me, get that way."

On October 24th, 1932 at Convention Hall in Camden, New Jersey, "Pink" Gardner successfully defended his World Light Heavyweight Title against Johnny Carlin in a two out of three falls match.

On November 27th, 1933, Gardner successfully defended his World Light Heavyweight Title against Joe Montana in New York City, New York.

The year 1933, Carroll and Eleanor Gardner had their first born, known as "Jerry", Carroll Altz Gardner, Jr., then in 1935, he fathered a daughter named Eleanor Lunn Gardner, and finally in 1937, a son named George Richard Lunn Gardner. It was in 1934, that Sheriff Gardner ran for Congress as a Democratic candidate in the 30th District. Although he swept Schenectady County, New York, he failed to capture Hamilton, Montgomery, and Fulton Counties, losing the election in his campaign for Congress.

On January 8th, 1934, Gardner defeated Paul Berlenbach at Madison Square Garden in New York City.

He lost his World Light Heavyweight Title to Joe Banaski in 1934 and was defeated by Charley Fischer in 1935, his last bout.

Carroll "Pink" Gardner, the World's Middleweight and Light – Heavyweight Champion, retired after 25 years as a professional wrestler in 1936 at age 42, winning 90 percent of an estimated 750 bouts, earning about $150, 000, his injuries being cauliflower ears, a cut eye from his Light – Heavyweight bout with John Kilonis, and a busted nose from his Light – Heavyweight bout with Carl Van Wurden.

After County Clerk George Bradt was convicted of felony larceny in the summer of 1936, "Pink" Gardner ran for office as "Mr. Democrat", but both parties looked at him as a hometown hero to Schenectady.

The Republican based *Schenectady Gazette* stated:
"Three years of his administration saw countless improvements in the sheriff's office. He revised and modernized both the legal and police bureaus of the department, installing businesslike methods and introducing an efficient system of county uniformed police. Inspectors and officials of the State Department of Correction declared in their reports that the conditions of the county jail and all bureaus of the sheriff's office here under Sheriff Gardner were surpassed in efficiency by no other county in the state.

In view of Mr. Gardner's excellent record for efficiency in the conduct of the sheriff's office during his three – year term, a strong wave of sentiment to draft him for the office of county clerk has swept the county..."

Carroll A. Gardner won the election as County Clerk of Schenectady County, New York in a landslide election. He took office on November 10th, 1936 and was the first Democrat since 1912 to hold that position. Gardner later was re – elected time and again, for ten consecutive terms, even being President of the New York State County Clerks Association.

It was during World War II that Gardner taught wrestling and jujitsu at the Marine barracks in Scotia, New York. After the war, the *Rotarian* magazine in December of 1949 stated: **"At 55, "Pink" Gardner – a member of the Rotary Club of Schenectady – is still "in the pink" and using leverage of a different sort to win a fall on the years. Turning time against itself, he is young both in body and in spirit."**

The former wrestling champion was also President of the New York State Retail Monument Builders Association during the 1950's; the first President of the Capitol District Retail Monument Dealer's Association, Inc.; and he was the National Director of the Monument Institute of America.

He set up his own monument in the Vale Cemetery before his death, the statue which says, "The Wrestlers". Gardner stated, **"In my wrestling career, I learned that success was based upon preparedness. I have never forgotten the lesson. Death is inevitable anyway, and I knew the type of tombstone I wanted, so I thought I would have it constructed."**

The inscription on Carroll "Pink" Gardner's tombstone reads, **"The basic rule for success is the heart to fight, the will to win, the ability to lose and, most of all, the spirit fight again."**

It was for a period of 30 years that he suffered from Paget's disease, but despite this, he ran for the Democratic nomination for Congress in the 32nd District, of course winning Schenectady County, but losing Fulton, Montgomery, and other counties.

He was awarded a trophy in 1963 which stated: **"Presented by the Mount Pleasant Athletic Club to Pink Gardner, Quarter Century Athlete of the Year"**, and **"To Pink, in appreciation for faithful and extraordinary service in behalf of Old Time Football Players Association."**

1924
1949

He's 55—and Still in the Pink!

INSOMNIA IS NOT INCLUDED IN THE VOCABULARY
OF THIS SCHENECTADY ROTARIAN WHO HAS 'LEVERAGE' ON LIFE.

WHEN Carroll A. Gardner, of Schenectady, New York, was light heavyweight wrestling champion of the world, he was a master of leverage. A tired opponent once grunted, "That guy turned me against myself. My own muscles beat me!"

At 55, "Pink" Gardner—a member of the Rotary Club of Schenectady—is still "in the pink" and using leverage of a different sort to win a fall on the years. Turning time against itself, he is young both in body and in spirit.

Don't get "Pink" wrong. He does not advocate a killing pace of physical exercise for the middle-aged man. Moderation is his key to health and happiness. "The gym and the golf course," he says, "should only be indulged to that point where a man feels a beneficial and exhilarating effect. More is too much."

When the age of 42 flashed past, Gardner suddenly realized he was no longer exhilarated by a workout in the professional ring. It was time to taper off.

"I had a long talk with myself," he says. "I knew to stop wrestling at 42 was dynamite. It meant reorganization of my entire physical and part of my mental life."

Gardner accomplished an even transition in a startling way. While wrestling he had been managing his own monument business. Over the building that housed this enterprise, he installed a complete public gymnasium. With daily workouts he began the tapering-off process. But it has never been completed, and he still spends an hour or two on the apparatus regularly every day.

In Summer this is modified with sun baths on top of the building while he eats his lunch of crackers and milk. The result is a physique comparable to what it was 25 years ago, a trim 175 pounds.

On the mental side Gardner was still restless. So, in addition to his monument works, he sought new outlets for his limitless energies. When World War II came along, he taught wrestling and his own version of jujitsu at the Marine barracks in Scotia, New York. Following the war he ran for the county clerk's job, and was easily elected, even though old-timers considered the opposing party to be "in solid."

Politics wasn't a new field for Gardner. He was sheriff of his county in the early '30s. During a raid on a gambling establishment, one of his deputies smilingly observed that the sheriff was just as good with an ax on a slot machine as he was with a step-over toe hold in the ring.

While sheriff, Gardner met and married Eleanor Lunn, daughter of the late George R. Lunn, onetime lieutenant governor of New York State.

The Gardners have three children, two boys and a girl. Their 14-year-old daughter is adept at outdoor sports, and Gardner already has begun instructing his 15-year-old in the techniques of wrestling. But the young lad is quick to admit that it will be some time before he is able to pin his dad.

How does Gardner keep it up? It's just a matter of leverage, he claims: sticking to a balanced program, with each job well done in its turn. A "cat napper" himself, he finds that his philosophy of life combined with regular exercise brings complete peace of mind, the world's best antidote for insomnia.

—BARNETT FOWLER

Unusual Rotarians

Carroll "Pink" Gardner died from a heart attack at age 75 at his home while in office in 1969 as County Clerk of Schenectady County, New York. He was a great storyteller, family man, and friend, one of those people loved by everyone. Gardner was a wrestler, sheriff, monument dealer, county clerk, and much more during his colorful career.

His son, "Jerry" Carroll Altz Gardner, Jr. was a swimming state champion, standing 6' 3, 210 pounds, and his son, George Richard Lunn Gardner was a newspaper reporter, editor, realtor, and former Mayor of St. Augustine, Florida, who had written a book titled, _The Schenectadians: The Story of Schenectady's 20th Century and Two Men Who Helped Shape It_, which tells the story of George Lunn and Carroll "Pink" Gardner.

A member of the Democratic Party read into record at the U. S. House of Representatives:

"He remained my friend and counselor. I knew him when I was just a boy and he was the new world's light – heavyweight wrestling champion, in the days before wrestling became more of an entertainment than a sport. He helped me get into the political life for the first time in Schenectady and I have always tried to emulate his consistent courage, his independence, and his consistent ability to put service to the community ahead of mere partisanship."

Barney Fowler, who had wrestled with him, drank with him, and campaigned with him, had written:

"Is that all there is? The song asks. And the answer is no…the song is, indeed wrong; that is not all there is, even tho' it is ended. A thousand more stories can be told about Pink Gardner and will be, and in this entire area, at least, he will become a legend."

A Parable of Immortality by Henry Van Dyke

"I am standing upon the seashore – a ship at my side spreads her white sails to the morning breeze and starts for the blue ocean. She is an object of beauty and strength, and I stand and watch until, at length, she hangs like a speck of white cloud, just where the sea and sky come down to mingle with each other.

"Then someone at my side says, 'There. She's gone.'

"Gone where? Gone from my sight – that is all. She is just as large in mast and hull and spar as she was when she left my side, just as able to bear

her load of living freight to the place of destination. Her diminished size is in me, not in her.

"And just at the moment when someone at my side says, 'There! She's gone,' there are other eyes watching her coming, and other voices, ready to take up the glad shout, 'There! There she comes!'

"And that is dying."

Carroll Altz "Pink" Gardner

Special thanks to the late George Richard Lunn Gardner

References:
The Schenectadians: The Story of Schenectady's 20th Century and Two Men Who Helped Shape It by George Richard Lunn Gardner

RULON GARDNER

Rulon Gardner, the Olympian, is the only American to ever win both the Olympic Gold Medal and the World title in Greco – Roman wrestling. He is a legend in his own time. Gardner is America's greatest wrestler to compete in the Olympic Games.

He is most famous for his 2000 Olympic Gold Medal for Greco – Roman wrestling which shocked the wrestling world when he defeated "the greatest wrestler of all time" Russian Aleksandr Karelin, who had remained undefeated for 13 years, Gardner's victory being one of the biggest upsets in sports history.

Rulon Gardner was the 2000 Olympic Super Heavyweight Greco – Roman Wrestling Gold Medalist and the 2004 Olympic Super Heavyweight Greco – Roman Wrestling Bronze Medalist.

Gardner was the 2001 World Super – Heavyweight Greco – Roman Wrestling Champion, the first and only man to win Olympic and World titles in Greco – Roman Wrestling in the Super – Heavyweight division.

Rulon Gardner was born on August 16th, 1971 in Afton, Wyoming, the youngest son of Reed and Virginia Gardner. He was raised on a dairy farm and attributes his physical strength to the physical labor of working on the family farm. His lineage dates back to Scottish immigrant Robert Gardner (1781 – 1855) of Renfrewshire, Scotland who settled in Salt Lake County, Utah.

His great – great grandfather was Archibald Gardner (1814 – 1902) who was one of the early Mormon settlers of Star Valley, Wyoming. He had 11 wives and 48 children, the father of 27 sons. Archibald Gardner's life is memorialized by a monument in Afton, Wyoming and a restored gristmill at Gardner Village, the site where he built his original flour mill in West Jordan, Utah.

Gardner was wanted by federal agents enforcing anti-polygamy laws and in 1886, he made a trip to California to visit his brother William Gardner. On his last trip, he evaded federal agents once again when he visited Mexico. He visited his brother Robert Gardner in southern Utah and in 1889, he established a home in Star Valley, Afton, Wyoming.

Archibald Gardner and his brother Robert Gardner

Rulon Gardner suffered from a learning disability and was often teased for being overweight in school. He attended Star Valley High School in Afton, Wyoming where he was a three-sport letter winner, standing out in football, wrestling, track and field. Gardner was an All-State selection in both football as well as wrestling.

Gardner was the 1989 wrestling state heavyweight champion.

He attended junior college at Ricks College (now BYU-Idaho) in Rexburg, Idaho. Gardner won the NJCAA national heavyweight wrestling championship. Afterwards, he earned a football scholarship to attend the University of Nebraska-Lincoln.

Rulon Gardner married and fathered a daughter named Stacey, but sadly on December 26th, 1990, the day after Christmas, she died in a terrible car accident.

He finished fourth in the 275 lb. weight class at the 1993 NCAA Championships, earning All-American honors. Gardner graduated from the University of Nebraska-Lincoln with a bachelor's degree in physical education. He attended both Ricks and Nebraska on wrestling scholarships.

As a member of Sunkist Kids (Cascade, Colorado) Rulon Gardner was the National Super – Heavyweight Greco – Roman wrestling champion four times at the U. S. Nationals and the World Team Trials.

He was the 1995, 1997, and 2001 U. S. Champion, earning the James E. Sullivan Award that year.

On September 24th, 2000, Day 10 of the Olympic Games in Sydney, Australia, Rulon Gardner, never an NCAA champion or world medalist, defeated Russian Aleksandr Karelin for the Super – Heavyweight Greco – Roman Gold Medal. Karelin was undefeated for 13 years. Rulon Gardner earned worldwide celebrity for his upset victory, being a hometown hero in Afton, Wyoming.

Then, at the 2001 World Championships in Patras, Greece, Rulon Gardner defeated Yuriy Yevseychyk of Israel and Georgive Soldadse of Ukraine in the preliminaries. Then in the quarterfinals, he drew with Russian Yuri Patrikeev. While down 3 – 0, Gardner went to the upperbody, threw and pinned Patrikeev at the five-minute mark.

Finally, in order to qualify for the finals, Gardner defeated World and Olympic medalist Sergej Moreyko of Bulgaria, 3 – 0, his five – match march to the title being one of the greatest U. S. Greco – Roman efforts in history.

Rulon Gardner defeated World Silver Medalist Mihaly Deak-Bardos of Hungary 2 – 0 in overtime for the World Championship Gold Medal in Greco – Roman wrestling, making him the first and only American to win both the Olympic gold medal and the World Championships gold medal.

He was the 2001 USOC Male Wrestler of the Year.

It was in 2003, he had his toe amputated and a dislocated wrist while in a snowmobile accident as well as a motorcycle accident.

Gardner competed in the 2004 Summer Olympics in Athens, Greece, earning the Bronze Medal. Afterwards, he placed his shoes in the middle of the mat as a symbol of retirement. Later, he was a host for a professional wrestling league called Real Pro Wrestling.

On New Year's Eve, December 31st, 2004, Rulon Gardner fought Judo Gold Medalist Hidehiko Yoshida in a mixed martial arts bout for the Pride Fighting Championships at an event named PRIDE Shockwave 2004 in which the experienced MMA fighter Hidehiko Yoshida faced the much larger Rulon Gardner who was trained by former UFC Heavyweight Champion Bas Rutten.

Gardner defeated Yoshida by 3 – Round Unanimous Decision in Saitama, Japan.

According to MMA champion fighters Dan Henderson and Randy Couture, Rulon Gardner punched harder than anyone.

On February 24th, 2007, Gardner and two other men survived a plane crash in Lake Powell, Utah. Afterwards, in January of 2011, at 6' 1, 474 pounds, Rulon Gardner was a contestant on season 11 of the American reality television show, *The Biggest Loser*.

Rulon Gardner has been a motivational speaker and coach for the Salt Lake City high school wrestling team.

He is the author of his autobiography (co-written by Bob Schaller) titled: *Never Stop Pushing: My Life from a Wyoming Farm to the Olympic Medals Stand.*

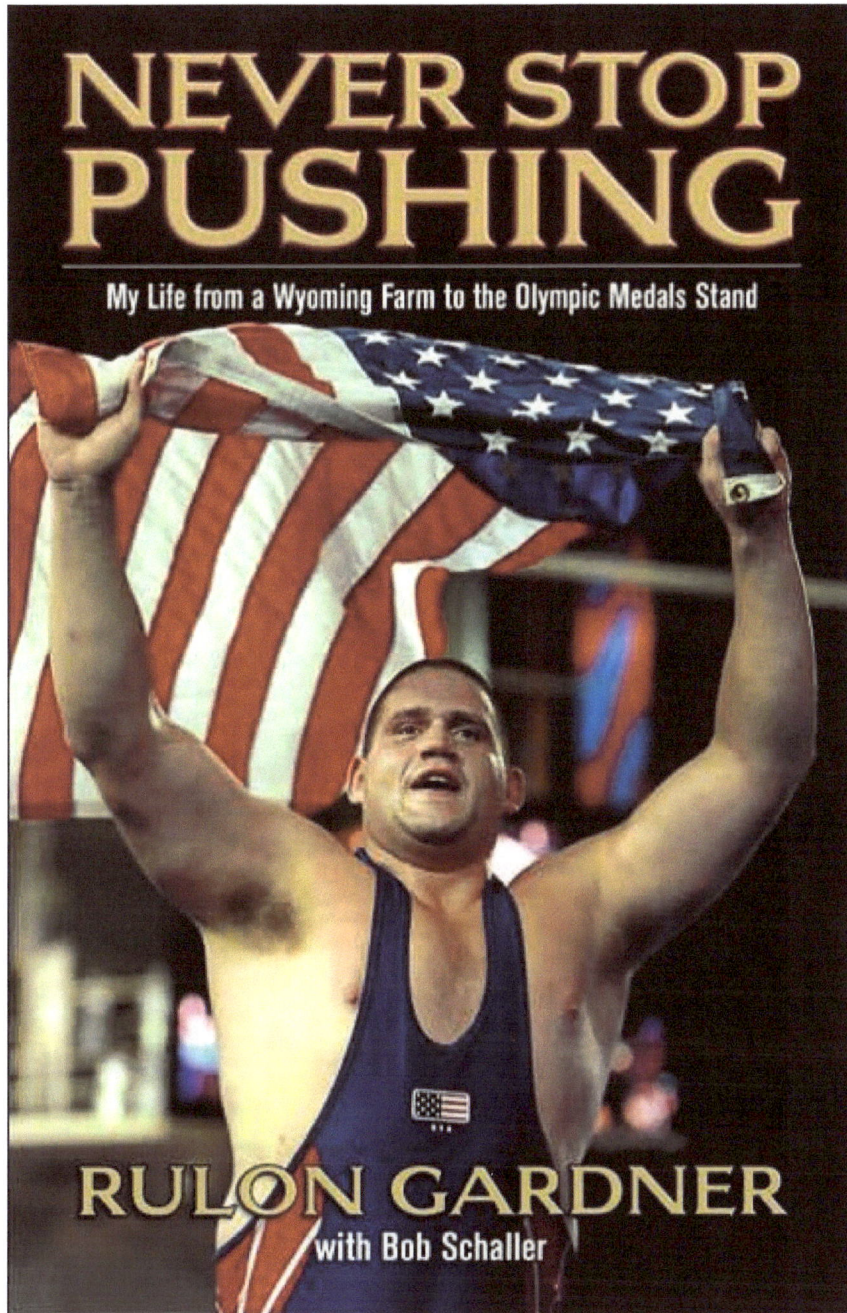

Rulon Gardner was inducted in 2010 as a Distinguished Member of the National Wrestling Hall of Fame and Museum.

Special thanks to Rulon Gardner

References:
Never Stop Pushing: My Life from a Wyoming Farm to the Olympic Medals Stand

Chapter IX: Politicians

"Excellence is doing ordinary things extraordinarily well." – John W. Gardner

GOV. HENRY GARDNER

Gov. Henry Gardner, the Governor of Massachusetts, was the 23rd man to take office. He was a member of the Whig Party and the Know Nothing Party. Gardner was a native of Massachusetts.

Henry Joseph Gardner was born on June 14th, 1819 in Dorchester, Massachusetts. His parents were Henry Gardner and Clarissa Holbrook Gardner. His grandfather was also named Henry Gardner, a Harvard graduate who was state treasurer from 1774 to 1782 in Massachusetts during the American Revolution.

As a young man, Henry Gardner was educated in private schools around Boston and attended Phillips Exeter Academy. Then after graduation he attended Bowdoin College and began his career as a dry goods merchant in Boston. Gardner married Helen Cobb of Portland, Maine, the couple having seven children.

He was part of the local Whig Party in the early 1850's as a moderate conservative Websterite, being elected to the Boston City Council until 1853, and in 1854 joined the movement of the Know – Nothing Party. His separation from the Whig Party involved their support of the pro – slavery Kansas – Nebraska Act. Afterwards in October of 1854, he was chosen as the Know Nothing gubernatorial candidate.

Gardner won by a landslide against Governor Emory Wasburn in November of 1854, becoming the 23rd Governor of Massachusetts.

He won 79% of the vote and the 1855 session was one of the most productive in the state's history with about 600 bills and resolutions being passed. Governor Gardner addressed the level of immigration reaching crisis proportions. He also omitted reform issues such as the ten – hour workday and avoided the subject of slavery.

It was during his three terms in office the Know Nothing Party made several changes to the state constitution, including replacement of majority voting with plurality voting.

Gardner defeated Republican Julius Rockwell in the 1855 election, and in 1857 re – election to Nathaniel Banks. It is interesting to note, Banks would become a Union general in the Civil War, fighting against a Confederate general named Franklin Gardner. Although, the Union Army won the Siege of Port Hudson, Louisiana, General Gardner inflicted heavy losses on the enemy, General Banks being outclassed.

On September 14th, 1869, his son F. W. Gardner shot and wounded J. R. Smedberg in a famous pistol duel in Sausalito, Marin County, California, being widely reported.

After Henry Gardner had lost re – election as Governor of Massachusetts, he continued his dry goods business until 1876 and in 1887 he became an agent for the Massachusetts Life Insurance Company.

He was recognized by Harvard University with honorary degrees and in 1855 was made a member of the Ancient and Honorable Artillery Company.

On July 21st, 1892, Henry J. Gardner died at age 73 in Milton, Massachusetts.

References:
Nativism and Slavery: The Northern Know Nothings and the Politics of the 1850s by Tyler Anbinder
The Transformation of Political Culture: Massachusetts Parties, 1790s – 1840s by Ronald Formisano
The Origins of the Republican Party, 1852 – 1856 by William Gienapp

HON. WASHINGTON GARDNER

Hon. Washington Gardner, the Republican, was a farmer, soldier, lawyer, minister, professor, and politician in the Republican Party. He served his country, practiced law, served his church, educated, and served in politics. Gardner led a life of service.

"Then came the figure on whom all eyes rested with respect. On a strapping prancing horse, Commander – in – Chief Washington Gardner, his black hat in hand, and his snowy hair glistening in the sunlight, was a picture of his beautiful old age as he rode ahead of his staff." – National Encampment Sept. 1914 GAR Reunion

Washington Gardner was born on February 16th, 1845 in Morrow County, Ohio to John Lewis and Sarah Goodin Gardner. He was the youngest of six children, being raised on a farm. His grandfather was John Gardner.

He enlisted in the Union Army as a private at age 16 in October of 1861 and served in Company D, 65th Regiment, Ohio Volunteer Infantry. Gardner earned the rank of sergeant and was wounded in action at the Battle of Resaca in Georgia. He was discharged in December of 1865 and began his education.

Gardner attended school at Berea, Ohio, then Hillsdale College in Michigan, graduating in 1870 from the Ohio Wesleyan University, Delaware, Ohio. He studied in the school of theology at Boston University until 1871 and in 1876 he graduated from Albany Law School. Gardner was admitted to the bar and began his practice in Grand Rapids, Michigan.

He entered the ministry of the Methodist Episcopal Church and served twelve years. Gardner was commander of the Department of Michigan, the Grand Army of the Republic in 1888, and from 1889 to 1894 he was a professor in Albion College. On March 20th, 1894, he was appointed Michigan Secretary of State by Governor John T. Rich, beginning his career as a politician.

Gardner was then elected twice to the position in 1894 and 1896, serving until 1899, the year before in 1898 defeating Democrat Albert M. Todd, being elected as a Republican from Michigan's 3rd congressional district to the 56th United States Congress. He was re – elected from 1899 to 1911 to five succeeding Congresses. Congressman Washington Gardner served as chairman of the Committee on Expenditures in the Department of Commerce and Labor in the 61st Congress.

It was at the National Encampment, GAR reunion for Union soldiers in September of 1914 in Detroit, Michigan, a parade was held in which Albion's Washington Gardner was the main attraction.

He was commander – in – chief of the Grand Army of the Republic from 1913 to 1914, then he unsuccessfully ran for Governor of Michigan. Then from March of 1921 to March of 1925, he served as Commissioner of Pensions. After an automobile accident, Gardner retired from public life.

Dr. Gardner wrote several books, his most well-known being titled, *A History of Calhoun County*, which was published in 1913 and was a two-volume set.

On March 31st, 1928, Congressman Washington Gardner, a leader of men, died at age 83 in Albion, Michigan, being buried at Riverside Cemetery. On April 1st, 1928, *New York Times* reported: **"Ex – Pensions Chief, Dr. Gardner, Dies. Was Representative From the Third Michigan District for Twelve Years. Former Head of G. A. R. Prominent in the Red Cross and in the Management of Homes for Children".**

As Albion's most distinguished citizen, Washington Gardner High School, now Washington Gardner Middle School, in Albion, Michigan is named in his honor.

Courtesy to Frank Passic for photograph of Washington Gardner.

References:
Biographical Directory of the United States Congress

SEN. AUGUSTUS GARDNER

Sen. Augustus Gardner, the Senator of Massachusetts, was a Republican congressman. He was an American patriot. Gardner served his country during the Spanish – American War and World War I.

Augustus Peabody Gardner was born on November 5th, 1865 in Boston, Massachusetts. His parents were Joseph Peabody Gardner and Harriet Sears Amory. He was a descendant of Thomas Gardner, the first Governor of Massachusetts.

He was also a nephew to John Lowell "Jack" Gardner II, the husband of art collector Isabella Stewart Gardner, both of whom adopted him and his brothers Joseph and William after the death of their parents.

Gardner graduated in 1886 from Harvard University and studied law at Harvard Law School, but never practiced.

On June 14th, 1892, he married Constance Lodge, daughter of Henry Cabot Lodge, a Republican congressman in Nahant, Massachusetts.

Gardner fought in the Spanish – American War as a captain and assistant adjutant general at the Battle of Coamo, serving from May of 1898 to New Year's Eve, 1898, surviving the war.

Then in 1899 he began his political career when he was elected as a member of the Massachusetts Senate as a Republican and was chairman of the Committee on Industrial Arts and Expositions during the Fifty – ninth and Sixtieth Congresses. It was at the beginning of World War I, his sister – in – law, Mrs. George Cabot Lodge along with her three children were stranded in France and in August of 1914, Gardner traveled abroad and had them brought to safety in London.

Gardner resigned from Congress in April of 1917 and entered the U. S. Army on May 24th, 1917 as a colonel in the Adjutant General's Department. He was assigned to the Eastern Department at Governors Island in New York Harbor and later as adjutant of the 31st Division.

As a warrior, Gardner desired combat duty and as requested, he accepted a demotion to the rank of major in December of 1917, being placed in command of the 1st Battalion, 121st Infantry, 31st Division in Camp Wheeler, Georgia.

However, he died on January 14th, 1918 from pneumonia while on active duty in Macon, Georgia, being buried in Arlington National Cemetery. Gardner was awarded in 1923 the Distinguished Service Medal and his award citation states: **"His entire service was characterized by untiring zeal, devotion to duty and marked success."**

References:

www.wikipedia.com
Gardner Memorial: A Biographical and Genealogical Record of the Descendants of Thomas Gardner, Planter, Cape Ann, 1624, Salem

GOV. MAX GARDNER

Gov. Max Gardner, the Governor of North Carolina, was the 57th man to take office. He was an informal advisor to President Roosevelt. Gardner was also chosen by President Truman to be ambassador to the United Kingdom.

"There is one in particular I would like to mention, however, and one I made Under Secretary of the Treasury, and I also appointed him to be Ambassador to Great Britain. He was a former Governor of North Carolina – Max Gardner – a wonderful man." – President Harry S. Truman, Address at the State Fairgrounds, Raleigh, North Carolina 1948

Oliver Maxwell Gardner was born on March 22nd, 1882 in Shelby, North Carolina. He was orphaned at a young age and attended North Carolina State University, then known as North Carolina A & M on a scholarship, majoring in chemical engineering. Gardner was involved in ROTC, played football, managed the baseball team, and served as the senior class president.

He was then selected by John Heisman, coach at Clemson for his All – Southern Team in 1903 and as a player he weighed 212 pounds. After graduation in 1903, Gardner later taught organic chemistry on campus. Then he enrolled at the University of North Carolina School of Law where he was also a football player.

Gardner was a distinguished football player and became one of the most respected members of The Dialectic and Philanthropic Societies at University of North Carolina at Chapel Hill, and was the only person to captain the football teams the North Carolina Tar Heels and the NC State Wolfpack.

Afterwards, he returned to Shelby, North Carolina where he practiced law. Then he married Fay Webb, daughter of politician Jas. L. Webb and niece to Congressman E. Yates Webb. It was then he entered the world of politics.

Gardner was elected as a Democratic state senator from Cleveland County, North Carolina, serving one term as President Pro Tempore of the North Carolina State Senate. He then served a term from 1917 to 1921 as the 13th Lieutenant Governor of North Carolina. Then in 1920, he lost the Democratic nomination for Governor, although it is thought the opposing side had used electoral fraud.

He took time off from politics and pursued business interests, including a textile mill.

Oliver Max Gardner was elected Governor of the State of North Carolina in 1928 and soon had to deal with the effects of the Great Depression within a year. He reorganized and reformed the state government while in office. Later, he took a pro – business and anti – union stance during the time of labor unrest, including the Loray Mill Strike.

He pushed through the legislature a workman's compensation law and mediated a massive 1932 strike of mill workers in the Greensboro – High Point area. Governor Max Gardner left office in 1933, governors of the state being restricted from seeking re – election at the time and afterwards, he practiced law and was a lobbyist in Washington, D. C.

Gardner served as an informal advisor and speech – writer for President Franklin D. Roosevelt who appointed him chairman of the advisory board to the Office of War Mobilization and Reconversion, later was a member of the Joint Anglo – American Commission on Palestine. President Harry S. Truman appointed him Under Secretary of the Treasury in 1946 and was also appointed to be ambassador to the United Kingdom. However, his successful career ended.

On February 6th, 1947, before ever arriving in London, Oliver Maxwell Gardner died at age 64 of coronary thrombosis at The St. Regis Hotel in New York City. He founded the "Shelby Dynasty" of politicians, controlling the North Carolina Democratic Party. Gardner – Webb University is named for him and his wife, as well as Gardner Hall at Appalachian State University and an economics building. The O. Max Gardner Award was established to recognize University of North Carolina system faculty, the UNC system's highest honor.

References:
www.GovernorOMaxGardner.com

JOHN W. GARDNER

John W. Gardner, the Reformer, was a man who improved the lives of millions of Americans through ideas and actions. He served as Secretary of Health, Education, and Welfare (HEW) and was the founder of Common Cause education program. Gardner was an American hero and a natural leader.

"John W. Gardner was the quintessential American hero; a man who transformed this nation through ideas and action that improved the lives of millions of Americans and shook up American politics. He was a leader, activist, author, and reformer."

John William Gardner was born on October 8th, 1912 in Los Angeles, California. He attended Stanford University and as an undergrad he set several swimming records and won Pacific Coast championships. Gardner graduated with great distinction earning a Ph.D. in Psychology at the University of California, Berkeley in 1938 and Dr. Gardner taught at Connecticut College. He also taught at Mount Holyoke and during the early days of World War II he was chief of the Latin American Section, Foreign Broadcast Intelligence Service.

Gardner, at age 30, entered the U. S. Marine Corps during World War II and was assigned as an intelligence officer to the Office of Strategic Services, known as O. S. S., precursor of the C. I. A., Central Intelligence Agency. He served in Italy and Austria. Gardner stated: ***"From my earliest years, I had thought of myself as a student, an observer, pleasantly detached from the mainstream of the world's action. From that point (the start of World War II) on, my life was to be governed by constant conflict between the life of action and the life of reflection."*** John Gardner in "There Was Light" (by Irving Shaw), 1970.

Afterwards, he joined the staff of the Carnegie Corporation of New York in 1946 and in 1955 he became president of this group and afterwards the Carnegie Foundation for the Advancement of Teaching. He also served as an advisor to the U. S. delegation to the United Nations, being a consultant to the U. S. Air Force in 1956 who awarded him the Exceptional Service Award. He was a trustee of the Metropolitan Museum of Art and of the Educational Testing Service and a director of the Woodrow Wilson Foundation. He served as chairman of the Rockefeller Brothers Fund Panel on Education and was chief draftsman of *The Pursuit of Excellence*.

He served on President Kennedy's Task Force on Education.

Gardner served as Secretary of Health, Education, and Welfare from August 18th, 1965 to March 1st, 1968, during the office of President Lyndon Johnson. He was a Republican serving a term in a Democratic president's time in office. Gardner oversaw significant expansions of the landmark Elementary and Secondary Education Act of 1965 which targeted funding poor students.

He received the Presidential Medal of Freedom in 1964 and the Public Welfare Medal in 1966 from the National Academy of Sciences, resigning as Secretary of HEW in March of 1968 not being able to support the war in Vietnam.

Gardner founded two influential national organizations: Common Cause and Independent Sector. He authors books improving leadership in American society and was the founder of two prestigious fellowship programs, The White House Fellowship and The John Gardner Fellowship at Stanford University and U. C. Berkeley.

He served on the Stanford University Board of Trustees from 1968 to 1982 and from 1968 to 1970, Gardner was chairman of the National Urban Commission.

It was in 1970, he was founding chairman of Common Cause, an educational program for those affected by poverty, and he also founded the Experience Corps.

He served on President Carter's Commission on an Agenda for the 1980s and later served on President Reagan's Task Force on Private Sector Initiative.

Gardner received the S. Roger Horchow Award for Greatest Public Service by a Private Citizen and from 1980 to 1983 he co – founded Independent Sector which lobbies on behalf of tax-exempt organizations.

He lent his name to the John W. Gardner Center for Youth and Their Communities at Stanford University in September of 2000, a center that partners with communities to develop leadership, research, and change to improve the lives of youth.

On January 20th, 1967, Gardner was featured on the cover of _Time_ magazine.

On February 16th, 2002, John W. Gardner died at age 89 from cancer in Palo Alto, California and was buried at the San Francisco National Cemetery.

Photograph is public domain.

References:
Excellence: Can We Be Equal & Excellent Too? (1995) by John W. Gardner
On Leadership (1994) by John W. Gardner

CHAPTER X: AUTHORS AND ENTERTAINERS

"There are only two plots in all literature: a person goes on a journey; a stranger comes to town." – John Gardner

ERLE STANLEY GARDNER

Erle Stanley Gardner, the Real Perry Mason, was the best – selling American author of the 20th Century at the time of his death. He was the creator and author of the most famous lawyer – detective stories known as "Perry Mason", making him the best American mystery writer of all time. Gardner was the real Perry Mason.

Erle Stanley Gardner was born on July 17th, 1889 in Malden, Massachusetts. His father was Charles Walter Gardner, descended from a long line of sea captains from Nantucket. His mother was Grace Waugh Gardner, and the family removed to California.

He graduated from Palo Alto High School in 1909 and enrolled at Valparaiso University School of Law in Indiana. After one month, he was suspended because of boxing, it being said he was kicked out for "slugging a professor". It is said he had taken on prize – fights while in California.

Gardner stated:
"I dodged the sheriff there, who was looking for me on telegraphed instructions from Valparaiso. I went out to the railroad camp and worked on railroad construction, a place so tough that no deputy sheriff would come anywhere near it. I worked there until the thing blew over…"

Afterwards, he attended Oxnard and worked for I. W. Stewart, then passed the California State bar exam in 1911 and on April 9th, 1912, he married a Mississippi native Natalie Frances Beatrice Talbert. They married while in San Diego and they had a daughter named Natalie Grace Gardner. It was then in 1917 he began his first law office in Merced but closed it after accepting a position working at a sales agency.

It was in 1923, during his spare time he began writing for pulp magazines, some calling him the "King of the Pulps", under names like Charles M. Green. Someone asked why his heroes always defeated villains with the last bullet in their guns. Gardner replied, **"At three cents a word, every time I say 'Bang' in the story I get three cents. If you think I'm going to finish the gun battle while my hero still has fifteen cents worth of unexploded ammunition in his gun, you're nuts."**

Then in 1921 he worked for Ventura firm Sheridan, Orr, Drapeau, and Gardner. As a lawyer, Gardner was an attorney – at – law for the Chinese, who called him **"t' ai chong tze"**, which means the "big lawyer". He remained there until 1933, but was bored by legal practice.

It was that year that his first book titled *The Case of the Velvet Claws* was published and the legend of Perry Mason was born.

Gardner stated:
"I dislike the routine practice of 'office law' and I keenly enjoy the trial of cases, particularly in front of a jury. So when I get homesick for a good old rough and tumble courtroom fight, I pull up my dictating machine and turn out another Perry Mason book."

He wrote 80 Perry Mason books, a total of 141 books, and 29 works by the A. A. Fair pseudonym, selling 170 million copies of his Perry Mason series. It was the greatest sales record of any fiction writer in the English language to that date. His postwar magazine contribution were nonfiction articles on travel, Western history, and forensic science.

The English novelist Evelyn Waugh in 1949 stated Gardner was the best living American writer.

It was from 1957 to 1966 that the television series *Perry Mason* ran and became a popular television series, Gardner even playing a part every now and then. He had separated from his wife in the 1930's and after her death in 1968, he married his long-time secretary Agnes Jean Bethell. Gardner had a fascination with Baja, California and wrote a series of nonfiction travel accounts of his explorations of the peninsula.

The Court of Last Resort was written in 1952 and earned Gardner his Edgar Award in the Best Fact Crime category. He devoted much time to "The Court of Last Resort", in collaboration with his friends in the forensic, legal, and investigative communities. The project reversed miscarriages of justice or malicious actions of police or prosecutors.

Gardner stated:

"I am an Honorary Texas Ranger with the rank of captain. I am a deputy in several counties in Texas. I have a diamond – studded star presented to me by the Texas Sheriffs' Association. The city trustees of Wichita, Kansas, appointed me an honorary chief of police of Wichita. I am a life member of the Kansas Peace Officers' Association. I am one of the one hundred Gold Star Deputies of Alameda County, California, and a deputy sheriff of Butte and of Riverside counties in California. I am an honorary member of the Fraternal Order of Police. I have spent a great deal of time patrolling with officers in radio cars. I have twice been invited to and attended Captain Frances G. Lee's seminars in homicide investigation at Harvard University. I am an honorary lifetime member of the American Polygraph Association, and I have a backlog of twenty – five years court – room experience as a trial lawyer....For the past thirty years I have been interested in homicide investigation and in police science. Some twenty – two years ago I helped organize the so – called Court of Last Resort, and from my experience with that organization, learned a lot about the investigation of crime."

Erle Stanley Gardner retired to his ranch where he had numerous collections and on March 11th, 1970, he died in Temecula, California, the best – selling American writer of the 20th Century at the time of his death.

"Erle Stanley Gardner, 1889 – 1970. No publisher ever had a more loyal author or a better friend." – Morrow Publishing

"...and while it may have been said of others, I believe it can be more sincerely said of Erle Stanley Gardner, that no matter what age he died, Erle Stanley Gardner died young." – *Erle Stanley Gardner: The Case of the Real Perry Mason* by Dorothy B. Hughes

It was in 2003 that a new school in the Temecula Valley Unified School District was named Erle Stanley Gardner Middle School.

Photograph courtesy to the New England Historical Society

References:
Secrets of the World's Best – Selling Writer: The Story Telling Techniques of Erle Stanley Gardner by Francis L. Fugate (1980)
Erle Stanley Gardner: The Case of the Real Perry Mason by Dorothy B. Hughes (1978)
The Case of Erle Stanley Gardner by Alva Johnston (1947)
Erle Stanley Gardner: A Checklist (1968)

MARVIN GARDNER

Marvin Gardner, the "Rudolf Valentino of the Philippines", was an actor who later served his country. He was known as "Eduardo de Castro". Gardner was once the most highly paid film director in the Philippines.

Marvin Edward Gardner was born on July 7th, 1907 in Sampaloc, Manila, Philippines. His father was William Henry Gardner, an American soldier from Tennessee who arrived during the Philippine Insurrection in 1899 and began serving as a police officer under the American administration. His mother was Caferina De Castro, a native of the Philippines.

Photograph of his father, William Henry Gardner, an American soldier turned Manila police officer.

William Henry Gardner had been a printer before he enlisted in 1899 in the 33rd Regt. U. S. V. Infantry, Co. I (The Texas Regiment) to fight in the Philippine War, earning the rank of sergeant and then served as a captain in the newly formed civilian police force in Manila.

Photograph of his paternal grandfather David Asbury Gardner.

The paternal grandfather was David Asbury Gardner, a carpenter by profession, born in 1850 in Tennessee, the son of a Confederate soldier. The Gardner family lived in Dyersburg, Tennessee. The elder Gardner died in 1922 from a heart attack, falling dead on the sidewalk in front of the Baker – Watkins store, being buried at the Fairview Cemetery in Dyersburg, Tennessee.

D. A. GARDNER,

ᴄONTRACTOR AND ʙUILDER.

Prompt and Careful Attention to all Kinds of Repair Work.

Marvin's grandfather David Asbury Gardner's business card as a contractor and builder in Dyersburg, Tennessee.

Photograph of his mother Caferina De Castro and Marvin as a boy.

Marvin Gardner worked on a freighter at sea that sailed for America. He became an actor in the early 1930s after joining a movie company. Gardner was handsome, being called the "Rudolf Valentino of the Philippines".

He used the professional name Eduardo de Castro (his mother's maiden name), and as his career flourished, Gardner married his leading lady Florence Little and the couple had two sons.

Florence Little and Marvin Gardner

However, they divorced and Gardner married Norma Krueger, having two children, one daughter, and one son.

It was in 1942, Marvin Gardner and his brother George fought in World War II. Manila was continually bombed. The Gardner brothers were guerrillas fighting in the hills, George evading arrest and returning home before liberation. However, Marvin was captured and imprisoned in the infamous Fort Santiago in Manila's walled city. After he was released, his family stated they could not recognize him with his beard and that he looked like a walking skeleton.

Gardner continued his career as a director and the movie *Zamboanga* (1938), which he directed, is considered one of the oldest extant Philippine films. However, he became an alcoholic and failed to produce films. His wife, Norma Krueger left him and his first wife, Florence tried to help him. However, he died broke and alone while working on a film titled *Maskara*.

On November 17th, 1955, Marvin Gardner died at age 48 from a stroke, due to a cerebral hemorrhage while in a hospital in Baguio City.

Courtesy to Robert Gardner for photographs and information

AVA GARDNER

"She was the most irresistible woman in Hollywood. Ravishing, fiery and dangerous, she had a smoldering beauty that awed even Liz Taylor and a sex appeal that led her into stormy marriages and affairs with millionaires and matadors. This is the story of her tempestuous life." – *People Weekly*

"She was the sex symbol who dazzled all the other sex symbols." – <u>Love Is Nothing</u> by Lee Server

"She can't sing. She can't act. She can't talk. She's terrific. Sign her!" - Louis B. Meyer

She was one of the great icons in Hollywood history--star of *The Killers*, *The Barefoot Contessa*, and *The Night of the Iguana*--and one of the few whose actual life was grander and more colorful than any movie. Her jaw-dropping beauty, charismatic presence, and fabulous, scandalous adventures fueled the legend of Ava Gardner--Hollywood's most glamorous, restless and uninhibited star." – <u>Love Is Nothing</u> by Lee Server

"She had this natural poignancy and her feelings ran very deep. To my mind she developed into a fine actress. I've been telling her that for years, and she always waves it off." – Gregory Peck

"She was exactly the opposite of the roles she played. She looked like a femme fatale and she wasn't. She was really sweet and dear and lovely..."
– Arlene Dahl

Ava Gardner, the Hollywood Movie Star, was one of the most beautiful women. She was once billed as the "Most Beautiful Animal in the World". Gardner was one of the top 100 legendary stars according to the American Film Institute.

"Elizabeth Taylor is not beautiful, she is pretty – I was beautiful." – Ava Gardner

Ava Lavinia Gardner was born on December 24th, 1922 in Grabtown, a small town in Johnston County, North Carolina. Her parents were Jonas Bailey Gardner and Mary Elizabeth "Mollie" Baker Gardner. Ava was born on a tobacco farm, but her father lost the farm due to debt and after the onset of the Great Depression, the family removed to Brogden School Teacherage, a boarding house for teachers.

Jonas Bailey Gardner, the son of a Confederate soldier, was described as **"long and lean, hawkish and handsome with green eyes and a cleft chin, brown-skinned on his face, neck, and forearms from the years spent working outdoors. He was a good man, temperate, loyal, hardworking."** – *Love is Nothing* by Lee Server

Her father operated a country store and sawmill, also performing maintenance at the Brogden School where his wife Mollie Baker Gardner cooked and cleaned. Afterwards, the family removed to Newport News, Virginia where they opened a boarding house for shipyard workers until 1936 with the death of her father from respiratory problems. Mollie Gardner removed her family back to North Carolina and in the summer of 1938 accepted a position as the matron of the Rock Ridge School Teacherage.

Ava graduated from Rock Ridge High School in 1939 and enrolled in Atlantic Christian College (now called Barton College) to study secretarial science.

Ava Lavinia was named after her father's younger sister, Ava Virginia.
Jonas and Mollie Gardner had seven children:
Beatrice Elizabeth "Bappie" Gardner Cole (1903 – 1993)
Elsie Mae Gardner Creech (1904 – 1987)
Edna Inez Gardner Grimes (1906 – 1981)
Raymond Allison Gardner (1908 – 1911) died in an accident
Jonas Melvin "Jack" Gardner (1911 – 1981) U. S. Army Infantryman and WWII Veteran, businessman, and member of North Carolina House of Representatives
Myra Merritt Gardner Pearce (1915 – 2005)
Ava Lavinia Gardner (1922 – 1990)

Ava's sister, "Bappie" was married to a professional photographer and living in New York City when Ava visited in the summer of 1941 and it was during the visit that Bappie's husband, Larry Tarr, took several photos of her. He displayed them in the windows of his studio. Someone suggested her photographs be sent to MGM if there might be interest in Ava becoming an actress.

Gardner and her sister "Bappie" arrived in August of 1941 in Hollywood, California. Ava's first film was *We Were Dancing* in 1942 which was followed by two years of bit parts. On January 10th, 1942, she married Mickey Rooney, but in 1943 they divorced only a year later.

Her name first appeared on a movie poster in 1944 for the film *Maisie Goes to Reno* and her career as a star began. It was in 1946, she starred with George Raft in *Whistle Stop.* She married band leader and jazz musician Artie Shaw in 1945, but the marriage ended the next year.

Ava Gardner in the 1953 film *Mogambo.*

Ava Gardner played the role of femme fatale Kitty Collins in the 1946 smash hit *The Killers.*

As a leading lady in Hollywood, Gardner played in such films as *Showboat* (1951), *The Snows of Kilimanjaro* (1952), *Lone Star* (1952), *Mogambo* (1953), *Knights of the Round Table* (1953), *The Barefoot Contessa* (1954), *Bhowani Junction* (1956), and *On the Beach* (1959) being an established star.

On Monday, September 3rd, 1951, at age 28, Ava Gardner was on the cover of TIME Magazine, the first woman from North Carolina to receive that honor.

It was that same year in 1951, she married famous singer and crooner Frank Sinatra, but in 1957 the marriage ended. They were one of Hollywood's famous couples. She also was involved with aviator and millionaire Howard Hughes, who once hit her, and she knocked him out with an astray.

She was honored to place her handprints and her footprints at Grauman's Chinese Theater in 1952 and in 1960 she received a star on the Hollywood Walk of Fame.

"What I'd really like to say about stardom is that it gave me everything I never wanted." – Ava Gardner

Gardner received her first and only Oscar nomination in 1953 for her role as Honey Bear Kelly in the film *Mogambo*. Afterwards, she won her first Box Office Blue Ribbon Award as Guinevere in *Knights of the Round Table* as well as three other movies. Gardner received three BAFTA (British Academy of Film and Television Arts) "Best Actress" nominations during her career: in 1957 for *Bhowani Junction*, in 1960 for *On the Beach*, and in 1965 for *The Night of the Iguana*.

She received a Golden Globe nomination for her role as Maxine in the film *The Night of the Iguana*.

Gardner moved to Spain in 1955 and while filming *Pandora and the Flying Dutchman*, she decided to leave Hollywood. She made seven films in twelve years, but in 1967 she received a large tax bill from the Spanish government. It was then she removed to London, England where she settled in a luxurious apartment at 34 Ennismore Gardens where she lived the rest of her life.

She made ten more films, her last film in 1983 being *Regina* and then appeared on a few television series for a short time before suffering from a stroke, leaving her partially paralyzed. Afterwards, she began to write her autobiography titled, <u>Ava: My Story</u>, but died before it was published. However, two writers finished the biography for her after her death.

On January 25th, 1990, the legendary actress Ava Gardner died at age 67 from pneumonia while at her home in London. She was buried at Sunset Memorial Park in Smithfield, North Carolina with her family. On February 12th, 1990, *People Weekly* magazine stated, **"AVA GARDNER, 1922 – 1990, THE LAST GODDESS"**.

She was also portrayed by actress Kate Beckinsale in the film *The Aviator*.

There is a statue of her in Tossa de Mar, Spain and in Smithfield, North Carolina resides the Ava Gardner Museum.

All photographs are public domain.

<u>References:</u>
<u>Love Is Nothing</u> by Lee Server
<u>Ava: My Story</u> by Ava Gardner
<u>Grabtown Girl: Ava Gardner's North Carolina Childhood and Her Enduring Ties to Home</u> by Doris Rollins Cannon
<u>Ava Gardner: A Bio – Bibliography</u> by Karin Fowler
Ava Gardner Museum
https://en.wikipedia.org/wiki/Ava_Gardner
http://www.avagardner.org/

JOHN EDMUND GARDNER

John Edmund Gardner, the Spy Novelist, was best known for his Ian Fleming's *James Bond* continuation novels, along with his series of *Boysie Oakes* books, most notably for his book titled, *The Liquidator*. He himself led an interesting life and career. Gardner was a Royal Marine Commando during World War II, an Anglican priest who lost his faith, later finding success for his spy and thriller novels, producing over 50 works of fiction.

"Gardner was a small – arms expert... [who] also knew a lot about explosives." – *"John Gardner; Thriller writer who revived Bond"*, Aug. 7th, 2007, Arnie Wilson, London, p. 35, *The Independent*

John Edmund Gardner was born on November 20th, 1926 in Seaton Delaval, Northumberland, England. His parents were Cyril Gardner, a London – born Anglican priest and Lena Henderson, a native of Seaton Delaval. It was in 1933 the Gardner family removed to Wantage in Berkshire where Cyril was Chaplain at St. Mary's while John was educated at King Alfred's School.

Gardner was a Royal Marine Commando, joining the Home Guard during World War II, despite being a teenager. He served in the Royal Navy Fleet Air Arm before transferring to the Royal Marines 42 Commando for service in the Middle East. Gardner was a small – arms expert who knew a lot about explosives, but described himself as "the worst commando in the world".

After the war he married Margaret Mercer, fathered two children, along with a third child from an affair, and he attended St. John's College in Cambridge to study theology, being ordained as an Anglican priest in 1953, but realized he had made an error on his career. He realized he had lost his faith during one sermon. Gardner stated: **"I didn't believe a word I was saying."**

He was released from the church in 1958 and became a drama critic with the *Stratford – upon – Avon Herald*. It was at age 33 he realized he was an alcoholic, drinking two bottles of gin a day. Gardner overcame his addiction and as part of his therapy, he began writing his first book in 1964, an autobiography titled, *Spin the Bottle*.

John Sutherland, a critic and scholar, stated of all the books Gardner published, it was **"the one that most deserves to survive"**.

Gardner began his career as a novelist in 1964 with *The Liquidator*, creating the character Boysie Oakes. Anthony Boucher of the *New York Times* had written, **"Mr. Gardner succeeds in having it both ways: He has written a clever parody which is also a genuinely satisfactory thriller."** The book was later made into a film.

After the success of both of his Oakes books, Gardner created a new character named Derek Torry, a Scotland Yard inspector of Italian descent. He also wrote three novels using the *Sherlock Holmes* character Professor Moriarty in a series titled, *Moriarty*. It was later was going made into a film titled, *The Return of Moriarty* but funding fell through before filming began.

It was in 1979 Glidrose Publications (now Ian Fleming Publications) approached Gardner and asked him to revive Ian Fleming's *James Bond* series of novels. It was between 1981 and 1996, Gardner wrote fourteen *James Bond* novels, leading to two Bond films. His novels received a mixed reaction from critics, but they were popular.

Several of his novels appeared in *The New York Times* Best Seller list bringing him commercial success. However, in the mid – 1990's he retired from writing Bond novels due to being diagnosed with esophageal cancer, Raymond Benson continuing the literary stories of the Bond novels. His break lasted for 5 years, his wife died, and after battling his illness he wrote a novel in 2000 titled, *Day of Absolution*. The Crime Writer's Association short – listed *The Liquidator*, *The Dancing Dodo*, *The Nostradamus Traitor*, and *The Garden of Weapons* for the annual Gold Dagger award.

Gardner removed his family to the United States in 1989 and was diagnosed with prostate cancer, then six years later with his esophagus. He was left nearly bankrupt due to medical expenses and in 1996 returned to the United Kingdom. Then he wrote a book titled *Bottled Spider* in which he introduced a new character Detective Sergeant Suzie Mountford, the name he took from Patricia Mountford, an ex – girlfriend, whom he later married. On August 3rd, 2007, John Edmund Gardner died at age 80 from heart failure in Basingstoke, England.

His list of Bond novels from 1981 to 1996 includes:
License Renewed
For Special Services
Icebreaker
Role of Honour
Nobody Lives for Ever
No Deals, Mr. Bond
Scorpius
Win, Lose or Die
License to Kill (1989) novelization of a film script
Brokenclaw
The Man from Barbarossa
Death is Forever
Never Send Flowers
SeaFire
GoldenEve (1995) novelization of a film script
Cold (1996) published in the United States as *Cold Fall*

References:
www.john-gardner.com

Courtesy to his son Simon Gardner

JOHN CHAMPLIN GARDNER

John Champlin Gardner, the "Literary Outlaw", was a controversial writer of his era; a novelist, poet, and teacher. He is most noted as the author of *Grendel*. Gardner was a bestselling American author, considered one of the greatest writers of all time.

"There are only two plots in all literature: a person goes on a journey; a stranger comes to town." – John Gardner

"John dared God to keep him alive." – Jim Gardner

"He could be a warrior in pursuit of his own principles." – Liz Rosenburg

"Very few writers, of any age, are alchemist enough to capture the respect of the intellectual community and the imagination of others." – Craig Riley

John Champlin Gardner, Jr., was born on July 21st, 1933 in Batavia, New York. His father was John Champlin Gardner, a lay preacher and dairy farmer while his mother, Priscilla Jones Gardner taught English at a local school. He was descended from Abial Gardner who served in the Rhode Island Militia as an artillerist during the American Revolution and it is said that his Gardner family descended from Sir Thomas Gardner, Knight.

As a child working on his father's farm in April of 1945, he was driving a tractor, accidently running over his younger brother Gilbert, resulting in his death, causing John to have nightmares and flashbacks. He later wrote a short story in 1977 titled _Redemption_. The incident haunted Gardner throughout his life.

On June 6th, 1953, he married Joan Louise Patterson, having children, but the couple divorced in 1980, twenty – seven years later.

Gardner attended DePauw University in Greencastle, Indiana and received his Bachelor's Degree in 1955 from Washington University in Saint Louis, Missouri. Afterwards, he received his Master of Arts and Doctor of Philosophy Degrees in 1958 from the University of Iowa in Iowa City, Iowa.

It was in 1966 he wrote his first fiction novel titled _The Resurrection_, afterwards _The Wreckage of Agathon_ and in 1970 he was the Distinguished Visiting Professor at the University of Detroit. It was in 1971 he wrote his famous novel titled _Grendel_, which is a retelling of the Beowulf saga from the monster's point of view. Gardner then wrote _The Sunlight Dialogues_ in 1972 and in 1974 _The King's Indian_.

It was in 1976 he wrote _October Light_ which was about an embittered brother and sister living with each other in rural Vermont, winning the National Book Critics Circle Award. Gardner wrote a literary criticism titled _On Moral Fiction_ in 1978 which caused controversy that excited the mainstream media in which he was critical of his contemporary fiction authors such as John Updike and John Barth. As a teacher of fiction writing, he wrote two books in 1983 on the craft titled, _The Art of Fiction_ and _On Becoming a Novelist_, both of which are classics.

John Gardner's thesis was that fiction should distinguish right from wrong.

American writer Gore Vidal found his novels pedantic and called Gardner the **"late apostle to the lowbrows, a sort of Christian evangelical who saw Heaven as a paradigmatic American university."** A student and future writer named Raymond Carver found Gardner inspiring as well as intimidating, who was kind as a writing mentor. It is also said that Gardner was a ladies' man and had a drinking problem.

He taught at Southern Illinois University at Carbondale. It was in 1977, he wrote a biography titled, _The Life and Times of Chaucer_. This was his only biography and he also wrote children's books.

It was in December of 1977 he was diagnosed with colon cancer and it was in 1980 he married poet and novelist Liz Rosenburg, but they divorced two years later. He served as professor at Harpur College of Binghamton University in Binghamton, New York, his last fictional work was titled, _Mickelsson's Ghosts_ in 1982 and he was working on _Stillness and Shadows_.

On Tuesday, September 14th, 1982, John Champlin Gardner died at age 49 in a motorcycle accident two miles from his home in Susquehanna County, Pennsylvania. The curve on Route 92 had been freshly – oiled gravel and Gardner was intoxicated, losing control of his 1979 Harley – Davidson motorcycle hitting the dirt shoulder, striking the guard rail and being thrown, the handlebars striking his abdomen. Gardner was pronounced dead at Barnes – Kasson Hospital in Susquehanna, Pennsylvania.

He was scheduled to marry his fiancé Susan Thornton four days before the crash and he was buried next to his brother Gilbert at Grandview Cemetery in Batavia, New York.

Susan Thornton later wrote a book in 2000 titled, _On Broken Glass: Loving and Losing John Gardner_.

Then in 2004, Barry Silesky wrote a biography titled, _John Gardner: Literary Outlaw_.

On September 14th, 2007, 25 years later after his death, _The New York Times_ headlined, **JOHN GARDNER, PUGILIST AT REST** by Dwight Garner, commenting on his literary criticism titled _On Moral Fiction_.

Photograph is public domain.

References:
On Broken Glass: Loving and Losing John Gardner by Susan Thornton
John Gardner: Literary Outlaw by Barry Silesky

COREY GARDNER

www.ingramcontent.com/pod-product-compliance
Lightning Source LLC
Chambersburg PA
CBHW042016090426
42811CB00015B/1658